BEGIN HERE

Jacques Barzun

BEGIN HERE

The Forgotten Conditions of Teaching and Learning

EDITOR: MORRIS PHILIPSON

*To remove ignorance is the sole duty of
the school. To fail in that battle when the enemy is
by nature inactive, when your troops are numbered in the
ten thousands, and when you have spent billions
on equipment is to suffer a stupid defeat.*

ADDRESS TO SCHOOL SUPERINTENDENTS, ASPEN, 1967

THE UNIVERSITY OF CHICAGO PRESS

Chicago and London

The University of Chicago Press, Chicago 60637
The University of Chicago Press, Ltd., London
© 1991 by The University of Chicago
All rights reserved. Published 1991
Paperback edition 1992
Printed in the United States of America
00 99 98 97 96 95 94 93 92   5 4 3

Library of Congress Cataloging-in-Publication Data

Barzun, Jacques, 1907–
Begin here : the forgotten conditions of teaching and learning /
Jacques Barzun ; editor. Morris Philipson.
p. cm.
Includes bibliographical references and index.
1. Teaching.   2. Learning.   I. Philipson, Morris H., 1926–
II. Title.
LB1775.B36   1991
371.1′02—dc20   90-25877

ISBN 0-226-03846-7 (cloth)
ISBN 0-226-03847-5 (paperback)

To Six Pioneers Who Fought
To Regain the Lost Ground:

. . . .

Arthur Bestor

Blouke Carus

A. Graham Down

† Banesh Hoffmann

† Mortimer Smith

† Charles C. Walcutt

Contents

Editor's Preface

For almost fifty years an intense if unsystematic self-examination about education has been going on in the United States, with different degrees of concern or despair; but apparently in the judgment of everyone involved, this self-examination continues to go on unsuccessfully. The pseudo-scientific proposals for all the remedies required have proved themselves no better than superstitions or crypto-magical incantations. They do not work. Still they are not the only proposals that have been made over the years. There now exists a body of clear thinking and sound pragmatic direction, i.e., exposition of what does work in *schooling* and Jacques Barzun is the preeminent advocate of those ideas. At last his most valuable essays—both analytic and instructive—are gathered together here in book form.

Jacques Barzun's experience, common sense, and spirited good humor clear the air of all the overheated nonsense and cut straight to the practical issues that something can be done about. It is on that level that he begins this work with the words "Forget EDUCATION. . . . Let us talk rather about teaching and learning."

He is not a newcomer to this ongoing debate over the hows and whys of education; he has been contributing to it for nearly fifty years. Of course, during those same years he has had other things to do. An original scholar and critic, he established himself as one of our outstanding cultural historians with such influential works as *Classic, Romantic, and Modern* and *Darwin, Marx, Wagner.* Later he produced two invaluable works of guidance — *The Modern Researcher* (with Henry Graff) and his own *Simple and Direct*—how-to books, aids to future scholars and writers in the development of their accuracy and effectiveness and elegance.

One early book, resulting from reflection on his experience in the classroom, *Teacher in America,* became a best seller and has remained in print steadily since 1945. *The American University* (1967) expresses his understanding of university administration after twelve years as Dean of Faculties and Provost of Columbia University. In speeches and articles, he has diagnosed the ills and would-be cures of what besets the American educational enterprise, but nowhere are those statements gathered together.

Engaged in writing a new work of history in 1990, Mr. Barzun was little disposed to edit the papers he had published on these topics, much less to write new introductions linking their main ideas to each other and to issues in the current debate on the reform of the schools. And he probably would not have done so but for my urging, pleading, and cajoling. In the end, with the papers grouping themselves into natural sequences, Mr. Barzun outdid even his customary good nature and wrote introductions—one to each essay—with his usual forthrightness and in his most "explicative and hortatory" manner. Taken together, the essays make clear that ten, twenty, forty years ago the problems of today were known and remedies were proposed by more than a few able observers. For example, the essay reprinted here entitled "The Educated Mind" originally appeared in a special issue of *Life* magazine dated October 16, 1950, and captioned "U.S. Schools: They Face a Crisis." The unhappy fact he points out is that we have known all along what should be done but have not done it—or have done the opposite.

To emphasize this truth, the editor has kept the fifteen pieces in their original form of articles or lectures, with only minor verbal changes; repetitions of some length have been removed, but brief allusive ones have been kept when they occur in different contexts, because they show the unity of the author's down-to-earth view of education and the relevance of his leading ideas to the many aspects of school work. These include: the reasons for poor teaching in math and science; the failure of "social studies"; the cure for dryasdust history; the damage done by multiple-choice tests; the pretentiousness of the art programs; the influence of television on the classroom; and—in higher education—the

causes of disarray in the curriculum and of the pointless faction-
alism among faculty and students.

The author maintains that his views are in no way "innovative," that he has never said or written anything about education
that people did not know before. That is the very point of his
advocacy: the answers to our school problems are there, known
of old. But we have preferred to ignore them, refused to act on
them, pursuing instead a host of false leads and so-called "innovative methods," even after it became clear that they led nowhere.

When he published his book *The American University* in
1967, Mr. Barzun predicted that the decline of "Higher Education" would not be reversed until somebody rediscovered what
Cardinal Newman called "the idea of a university"; and in the final
pages of that book he listed sixty-eight points on which reform
was imperative. All of those conditions remain the same twenty-
three years later. The failure has only been worsened by group
hostility and racial violence on campuses, and mounting tuition
fees for less and less educational benefit.

By giving under their titles the information about the original form and publication of these statements, the editor means to
underscore one of Mr. Barzun's contentions, that for thirty years
educationists have chosen to be deaf and blind to certain facts;
they were warned of the decay of the schools long since, and by
more than one voice. Hence Mr. Barzun's dedication of his book
to six pioneers. But of course he was there in addition to them.
These fifteen chapters, among other pieces of his, show that he
and his fellow pioneers were not unheard but unheeded. One of
these speeches was delivered not to a local club but to a convention of fifteen thousand teachers in Houston. The definition of the
educated mind was not a private musing but appeared in that special issue of *Life* when it was estimated that the periodical reached
20 million readers. Barzun's attack on multiple-choice tests came
out in the *New York Times;* he addressed gatherings of school superintendents and seminars in teachers' colleges. That these
speeches or articles were repeatedly picked up and reprinted by
other periodicals shows the extent of the interest taken in them at
the time. Yet contemporary concern among teachers, parents, and

the general public brought no change. Now that the whole country is aroused—governors, foundations, columnists, school boards—why imagine that common sense might help rescue our schools during the decade to come? I can think of two reasons.

One is that the situation is worse now than at any time in the past half-century, and, therefore, it is just possible that both the policymakers ("educationists") and teachers on the front line may be willing to rethink their ways and redirect the effort required for the achievement of their goals by beginning from scratch, by "beginning here." They have exhausted all hope of shortcuts, gimmicks, mechanized methods—in effect all the devices and ploys by which they were misled into believing some fancy new technique would do the job for them. Perhaps now they see no alternative but to recharge their good intentions with the belief that hard work alone will make things come out as they should.

The other reason is that this body of diagnosis and prescriptions from a true believer in teaching and learning achieves a "critical mass" in book form that these arguments did not have on their separate occasions. At any rate, here are facts and ideas that sensible people who have children in school, sons and daughters in college, will recognize as relevant and persuasive. Let such people carry the fight into their communities, acting on the principle with which our author ends one of his harangues: "It is always time to stop repeating the wise sayings and begin to believe them."

MORRIS PHILIPSON
Director
University of Chicago Press
Thanksgiving Day, 1990

FIRST THINGS

1

Schooling No Mystery

Forget EDUCATION. Education is a result, a slow growth, and hard to judge. Let us talk rather about Teaching and Learning, a joint activity that can be provided for, though as a nation we have lost the knack of it. The blame falls on the public schools, of course, but they deserve only half the blame. The other half belongs to the people at large, *us*—our attitudes, our choices, our thought-clichés.

Take one familiar fact: everybody keeps calling for Excellence—excellence not just in schooling, throughout society. But as soon as somebody or something stands out as Excellent, the other shout goes up: "Elitism!" And whatever produced that thing, whoever praises that result, is promptly put down. "Standing out" is undemocratic.

This common response is a national choice, certified by a poll: we have a self-declared "Education president." Good. But what happened soon after he took office? His popularity rating went up when it was discovered that he was less than articulate on his feet. One commentator said in a resigned tone, "It's not pretty, but it works." It works only because of our real attitude toward "excellence"—we won't have it.

Why should children make an effort to shine in school when shining is a handicap? Shining, that is, in school*work*. In athletics, it's another story. We do not cheer the duffers; there is no cry of elitism near the playing field. We pay large sums to get the best and to see that it is duly praised. Never mind what the school superintendent is like, we need a first-class coach and a good

3

band. The people who insist on all this and supervise it very effi-
ciently are those ultimately in charge of the schools, the schoolboards, and behind them are the general public who want to enjoy
exciting games and have their town excel.

The first question to settle, therefore, is the one asked repeatedly in the current debate about the country's system of public
instruction: "What do we really want from our schools?" The state
legislatures have been passing an unprecedented number of bills
to make things better, but improvement is not in sight. As one
observer said of the assembled Governors' draft for reform:
"Laudable goal, vague blueprint." Seventy-five percent of college
instructors report that students come to them unprepared; the
world of business talks of "a work force unqualified;" *Fortune*
magazine speaks of the schools' "impending collapse."

Given the public's muddled feelings about brainwork
(which is what "excellence" refers to) and the parental indifference up to now about what their children are being taught, the
school has a double fight on its hands: against ignorance inside the
walls and against cultural prejudice outside, the prejudice lying so
deep that those who harbor it do not even know they do. It none
the less tells the young what is really important. The result for
them is that learning, homework, teachers, tests, grades, standards, promotion form a great maze—mostly make-believe—
that they have to stumble through in order to be let go at last and,
thanks to a piece of paper, get a job.

Of course, some go on to college—as many as 58.9% of
high school graduates in 1988 were in college or on the point of
entering. But with some exceptions, their experience there will
not differ greatly. So-called higher education repeats the lower in
form and substance: the sole aim is "to qualify." Teaching is at a
low ebb and the curriculum is but a chef's salad of information,
much of it trivial. The best consists of technical training in the
specialties of the day.

As for the means of learning and thinking, that is to say,
reading and writing, the colleges are at the same point as the grade
schools—helpless in the face of illiteracy. The exceptional
teacher is still trying in graduate school to get decent writing and
intelligent reading out of his bright students.

For they are bright, and healthy, and the unworldly are eager for something better than they are getting, or got earlier during twelve mortal years. How did this great imposture come about? Through more than one cause, naturally. Perhaps the main one is the disappearance of the motive that established free schooling in the first place, 150 years ago: the intention was to give everybody a chance to improve his lot in life. Learning to read, write, and count meant equal opportunity. Lincoln, as everybody knows, had to teach himself. Now, with machine industry, the conditions of economic life have changed, and the illiterate somehow manage to get on, since we are told there are 60 million of them.

What is equally extraordinary is that good schools do exist, here and there, even and especially in the inner cities. "P.S. 94 "Somehow Making It" and "How Two Brooklyn Schools Can Be So Different!" These cries of amazement tell how far the public mind has fallen from its self-assurance of sixty years ago, when the largest cities had the best school systems and the nation as a whole felt a legitimate pride in its unique creation: the free public high school. Its graduates were equipped not only to perform well in the marketplace; they had also been given the means of growing intellectually, of becoming "educated." For they had acquired the basis of further learning by mastering a group of required subjects and, well before that, had been taught how to read, write, and count. Now the bewildered authorities are struggling to reach that earliest and simplest of abilities.

If they are teachers, these authorities now have to face the fundamental tasks that have been clouded over for half a century or more by pernicious doctrine. In the name of progress and method, innovation and statistical research, educationists have persuaded the world that teaching is a set of complex problems to be solved. It is no such thing. It is a series of *difficulties*. They recur endlessly and have to be met; there is no solution—which means also that there is no mystery. Teaching is an art, and an art, though it has a variety of practical devices to choose from, cannot be reduced to a science.

The present shortage of teachers, which has brought about the admission of college graduates *without* indoctrination in "methods," is an opportunity not to be missed. Liberal arts majors, if their courses were truly liberal, will be free of crippling ideas about how to teach. They will know their subject, they will think about *it* and not some "strategy," they will not believe the absurd dogma that there is no transfer in learning ability from one subject to another. They will deal with learning difficulties in the light of their own experience and not be so ready to ascribe them to "attention deficit" (located in the inner ear) or dyslexia, or home conditions, or lack of self-esteem. Teachers who can get their pupils to do well find that pride in performance overcomes many things, whereas failure and boredom bring on self-disgust as well as physical symptoms.

The generality that knowing a subject and wanting to teach it are the chief prerequisites to success in the profession suffers exceptions, of course. One of them is that dealing with small children in the preschool years does benefit from special training of a psychological kind. But even that is subject to a reservation, which rests on the fact that millions of mothers, without training, have taught their infants how to read and write. Still, where right intuition is lacking, textbook advice may help. But as soon as the child is old enough to interpret correctly what is simply said, the need for special diplomacy ends. A proof of this is that when older pupils are asked to teach younger ones—as has happened many times in history—their success is often remarkable. They understand the difficulties they themselves have undergone, just as the good teacher does.

That relation of age and of memory is indeed the one to be relied on in the present enlisting of college graduates to rescue the system from its foundering in a sordid blend of despair, violence, and illiteracy. This help comes just in time. For here and now other things than literacy are likely to perish with it. It was a liberal arts undergraduate named Woodrow Wilson who said, at a time when the public school was still a new American wonder: "Our liberties are safe until the memories and experiences of the past are blotted out . . . and our public school system has fallen into decay."

Teacher in 1980 America:
What He Found

· ·

Preface to the Third Edition of *Teacher in America*;*
New York Review of Books, Novemember 5, 1981;
One Hundred Great Modern Essays, Bobbs Merrill,
Indianapolis, 1983

To those who follow the news about education, the present state of American schools and colleges must seem vastly different from that described in this book.** Thirty-five years have passed, true; but the normal drift of things will not account for the great chasm. The once proud and efficient public-school system of the United States—especially its unique free high school for all—has turned into a wasteland where violence and vice share the time with ignorance and idleness, besides serving as a battleground for vested interests, social, political, and economic. The new product of that debased system, the functional illiterate, is numbered in millions, while various forms of deceit have become accepted as inevitable—"social promotion" or passing incompetents to the next grade to save face; "graduating" from "high school" with eighth-grade reading ability; "equivalence of credits" or photography as good as physics; "certificates of achievement" for those who fail the "minimum competency" test; and most lately, "bilingual education," by which school subjects are supposedly taught in over ninety languages other than English. The old plan and purpose of teaching the young what they truly need to know survives only in the private sector, itself hard-pressed and shrinking in size.

Meantime, colleges and universities have undergone a comparable devastation. The great postwar rush to college for a share in upward mobility and professional success was soon encouraged and enlarged by public money under the G.I. bills and the National Defense Education Act. Under this pressure higher educa-

*Liberty Press, Indianapolis, 1980. (Ed.)
**Refers to the original edition, Little Brown, Boston, 1945.

tion changed in quality and tone. The flood of students caused many once modest local colleges and deplorable teachers' colleges to suddenly dub themselves universities and attempt what they were not fit for. State university systems threw out branches in cities already well provided with private, municipal, or denominational institutions; and new creations—junior colleges and community colleges—entered the competition for the student moneys and other grants coming out of the public purse. The purpose and manner of higher education were left behind.

True, some of the novelties were beneficial. The junior and community colleges, with their self-regarding concern for good teaching, often awakened talent in students overlooked in the scramble for admission to better known places. But at all institutions, old and new, the increase in numbers requiring expansion—wholesale building, increase of staff, proliferation of courses, complex administration, year-round instruction—brought on a state of mind unsuited to teaching and learning. In their place, the bustle became a processing and being processed.

This deep alteration went unnoticed in the excitement of change and growth. But other influences soon made clear that the idea of college and university as seats of learning was being lost. Because of its evident social usefulness in war and peace, the academic profession after 1945 enjoyed two decades of high repute. The public no longer regarded "the professor" with distant respect for remote activities, but gave cordial admiration as between men of the world. The result was the introduction on the campus of a new standard of judgment. Scholars and scientists who had done something acknowledged by the outside world were a source of renown to the institution; they were the men who could bring to the campus lucrative research projects; they were valuable properties like top baseball players. And since every college and university was "expanding to meet social needs," these men were haggled over by rival places like artworks at an auction. The terms offered showed in dollars their value as bringers of prestige, and in "free time for research" the new conception of what an academic man was for. In the upward bidding between alma mater and the raiding institution it was not unusual to reach an offer guaranteeing "no obligation to teach" or (the next best thing) "leave of absence every other term."

Thus was the "flight from teaching" made explicit and official and nationwide. It had begun well before the war, during the Roosevelt years, when Washington drew on academic experts for help in administering the New Deal. But in those early days a scholar so drafted was expected to resign his university post after a one- or two-year leave. During the war this requirement would have seemed unfair, and so the custom grew of using the university as a permanent base for far-flung excursions. The large private foundations encouraged the practice and were not resisted: how could one retain these prize men on the faculty if they were denied the opportunities of high research? A large foundation can subsidize work in ten, twelve, twenty departments simultaneously, and protest would come from them all if the policy were established of chaining the professor to the classroom. The leave of absence—the absence itself—became the sign of the really able.

This new behavior forced on the academy could be called a species of colonialism on the part of the foundations and the government. Bringing money, they obtained areas of influence and exerted control without rights; their favor was sought and cherished; and they obviously diverted the professorial allegiance from the university to the outside power. With a dispersed, revolving faculty, the institution ceased to have a recognizable individual face. At the same time, the federal or foundation rules under which grants were made introduced a new bureaucratic element into the customary ways of academic self-governance. And this too changed the academic atmosphere for the worse. Under the double strain of expansionism inside and colonialism outside, the university lost its wholeness (not to say its integrity) and prepared the way for its own debacle in 1965–68.

The unresisted student and faculty riots of those years were the logical counterpart of unfulfilled promises. Brought up in the progressive mode of the lower schools, young people eager for higher learning—and others, indifferent but caught in the rush—found themselves on campuses where teaching was regarded as a disagreeable chore: students were an obstacle to serious work. Teaching was left to those few who, having seen it, still believed in it, and to those others who could not "get an offer" from elsewhere or a grant from Croesus public and private. Since such derelicts were not directing teams of research associates in studies of current social questions, or traveling on mission to settle the problems of Appalachian poverty or Venezuelan finance, there was nothing for them to do but teach. And much of this teaching was excellent, as is shown by the gratitude of many who took their degrees in those years.

But the prevailing mode was that of neglect and it bore hard on students, at a time when every kind of desirable occupation was becoming the subject of an academic course leading to a certificate. The "credentials society" was in full development and the need for high marks and glowing recommendations was imperative. When so-called teachers left in mid-semester or steadily missed office hours or showed their lack of interest in class or conference, they bred emotions likely to explode in future. Quite apart from the threat of the draft for the war in Vietnam, student feeling by the midsixties was one of open disaffection from the university and its faculty and from the society and its culture.

These last two objects of resentment were bound to fill the student mind when their mentors were so loudly diagnosing and dosing the ills of the world. As for the hatred of high bourgeois culture, it was communicated by nearly every contemporary novel, play, painting, or artist's biography that found a place in the popular part of the curriculum. So the age was past when freshman year in a good college came as a revelation of wonders undreamed of, as the first mature interplay of minds.

Moreover, in the new ambulant university, what might have been fresh and engrossing was presented in its least engaging form, that of the specialist: not Anthropology as a distinctive way of looking at peoples and nations, with examples of general import, but accumulated detail about a tribe the instructor had lived with—and apparently could not get away from. At best, the announced "introductory course" did not introduce the subject but tried to make recruits for advanced work in the field. This attitude no doubt showed dedication of a sort. It was easier to bear, perhaps, than the indifference of other professors who, in the name of the discussion method, let the students "exchange ideas" without guidance or correction—each class hour a rap session. But in none of these forms could the exercise be called undergraduate teaching; and its parallel in graduate school was equally stultifying to the many who in those years went on, hoping against hope, to obtain higher learning from institutions claiming the title.

The violent rebels against boredom and neglect, make-believe and the hunt for credentials never made clear their best reasons, nor did they bring the university back to its senses; the uprising did not abate specialism or restore competence and respect to teaching. The flight from the campus did cease, but that was owing to the drying up of federal money and the foundations' partial retreat from world salvation by academic means. What the upheaval left was disarray shot through with the adversary spirit. It expressed itself in written rules arrived at by struggle and compromise, through committees and representative bodies set up as the arena of divergent needs and claims. Students, faculties, and administrators tried to rebuild in their own special interest the institution they had wrecked cooperatively. But, alas, the duty to teach well cannot be legislated.

The result, fostered by a fresh wave of government regulation and supervision in favor of women and ethnic groups, was predictable. Colleges and universities have become bureaucracies like business and government. To defend its life against its envious neighbors, against City Hall, the state, and Washington, as well as against militant bands and individuals within, the academy obviously needs officials of the bureaucratic type; and their attitude inevitably spreads throughout the campus by contagion. In these conditions the old idea of *membership* in the university is virtually impossible to maintain. It is not compatible with corralling forces for contentious action and the jealous vindication of stipulated rights.

Nor are these sentiments sweetened by the present state of perpetual penury. Inflation makes balancing the budget a heroic annual act, which can only be done at the cost of some scholarly or educational need. Often, bankruptcy is averted only by acrobatic bookkeeping. And while the cost of tuition goes up, student enrollments go down—partly because of the population decline, partly because there are too many colleges, partly because industry and other unadvertized agencies have come to provide in many fields a training parallel to the schools'.

In this matter of enrollments, the colleges and universities were badly misled by statistics public and private. In the sixties, state and federal departments predicted a great surge of students by 1975. Many institutions responded by still more building, still more courses to prepare the future teachers of these expected hordes. Today, it is estimated that there are 125,000 Ph.D.'s without a post—and many others, long on tenure, but with few or none to teach.*

A great opportunity was missed after the time of troubles. Chaos and the will to reform gave the chance to recast the American college and university into simpler ways, intellectually sounder and more in keeping with its new material conditions. Simplicity would have meant not just giving up grants and foundation playthings such as "institutes" and "centers" for immediate social action, but also many ornamental activities, including public sports. Some of us who urged the move at the time were ridiculed as "scholastic-monastic," but I accept the phrase as tersely descriptive of a still desirable direction. "Monastic" here has of course nothing to do with religion or asceticism or the muddle of co-education and cohabitation now part of campus life. It betokens merely the mind concentrated on study in a setting without frills. To rediscover its true purpose is always in order for an institution or any other being, and doing so entails scraping away all pointless accretions. It is always a painful act, but it is least painful after a catastrophe such as happened in '65-'68.

The new direction would have had to be taken by several institutions in concert. They would have been criticized and misrepresented and denounced in the ordinary heedless way. They might even have suffered a few lean years; but with reduced tuitions and a shorter, clearer, and solider curriculum; with enhanced teaching and voluntary scholarship (as opposed to the publish-or-perish genre); with increased accessibility to the gifted poor, they

* "Today" refers to the year 1980. (Ed.)

would soon have earned respect and a following—a following of the best, by natural self-selection; after which, public support in money would have flowed to them by sheer economic preference.

Instead of that transformation we have but ruins barely concealed by ivy. For students, not the monastic life, but a shabby degradation of the former luxury; not the scholastic life, either, but a tacitly lowered standard, by which instructors maintain their popularity rating on the annual student evaluation, and the students thereby ensure the needed grades in the credentials game. For the faculty, salaries dropping faster under the inflation that also raises the costs of operation and tuition. For the administration, nothing but the harried life among demands, protests, and regulations. To expect "educational leadership" from men and women so circumstanced would be a cruel joke.

The manifest decline is heartbreakingly sad, but it is what we have chosen to make it, in higher learning as well as in our public schools. There, instead of trying to develop native intelligence and give it good techniques in the basic arts of man, we professed to make ideal citizens, supertolerant neighbors, agents of world peace, and happy family folk, at once sexually adept and flawless drivers of cars. In the upshot, a working system has been brought to a state of impotence. Good teachers are cramped or stymied in their efforts, while the public pays more and more for less and less. The failure to be sober in action and purpose, to do well what can actually be done, has turned a scene of fruitful activity into a spectacle of defeat, shame, and despair.

If both halves of the American educational structure have fallen into such confusion during the years since this book came out, what is the use of reading it now?—a legitimate question, which I asked myself when the present reissue was proposed to me. As I pondered, the proposers pointed out that except for a few months the book had been continuously in print since publication in that bygone age. The fact meant that it still reached several thousand new readers each year. By this empirical test, it must have some use, though years and numbers did not tell what it was.

I can only think that the book is read because it deals with the difficulties of schooling, which do not change. Please note: the difficulties, not the problems. Problems are solved or disappear with the revolving times. Difficulties remain. It will always be difficult to teach well, to learn accurately; to read, write, and count readily and competently; to acquire a sense of history and develop a taste for literature and the arts—in short, to instruct and start one's education or another's. For this purpose no school or college or university is ever just right; it is only by the constant effort of its teachers that it can even be called satisfactory. For a school is the junior form of a government and a government is never good, though one may be better than the rest.

The reason is the same in both cases: the system must create—not by force and not by bribes—some measure of common understanding and common action in the teeth of endless diversity. A government deals mainly with divergent wills, a school with divergent minds. Both try to generate motive power by proposing desirable goals. But all these elements are fluid, shifting, barely conscious, mixed with distracting, irrelevant forces and interests. And just as there are few statesmen or good politicians who can govern, so there are few true teachers and no multitude of passable ones.

If this book serves in any degree to make these generalities concrete and intelligible, then it has value in the present, when they seem so largely ignored or forgotten. I have been told a good many times by different persons that the reading of this book helped determine their choice of teaching as a career. On hearing this I always express regret—not because I believe the life of teaching a misfortune, but because it is an unnatural life. Again like governing, teaching is telling somebody else how to think and behave; it is an imposition, an invasion of privacy. That it is presumably for another's good does not change the unhappy fact of going against another's desire—to play, whistle, or talk instead of listening and learning: teaching is a blessing thoroughly disguised.

And yet we cannot do without teaching—or governing. We see right now all around us the menace of the untaught—the menace to themselves and to us, which amounts to saying that they are unselfgoverned and therefore ungovernable. There is unfortunately no method or gimmick that will replace teaching. We have seen the failure of one touted method after another. Teaching will not change; it is a hand-to-hand, face-to-face encounter. There is no help for it—we must teach and we must learn, each for himself and herself, using words and working at the perennial Difficulties. That is the condition of living and surviving at least tolerably well: let us say, as well as the beasts of the field, which have instruction from within—and no need of this book.

2

The Alphabet Equals the Wheel

The public and the press have been acting like incurables in despair and looking for a nostrum. The driving cause was briefly put in a headline: Work Force Fails To Meet Needs of Business; and again: Funding Goes Up, Scores Go Down. The scores are those of reading ability, local, state, and national, which nowadays are watched like the stockmarket. And daily also new patent remedies appear: "The Right to Read," "Technology Makes Better Teachers," "A Reading Recovery Project," " 'Spell As You Please': Surprising Results," and so on through acres of gimmickry.

All the schemes profess to overcome a monumental deficiency: the young are not learning to read. The number of illiterates is climbing toward a majority of the population and at this rate we shall soon be back at the early ages of literacy, when only a small caste could read and write—a true elite, and thus able to govern the rest.

The general anxiety is fit retribution for the 50-year folly of the look-and-say method of teaching reading, coupled with the assumption that the children of the poor, the black, and the Hispanics cannot learn. Being "disadvantaged" is now thought to be an insurmountable bar to learning.

That is criminal nonsense. All children can learn and do learn. By the time they first go to school they have learned an enormous amount, including a foreign language, since no language is native to the womb. So if they stop learning when in school, it must be because the desire to learn is killed by pro-

16

tracted non-achievement and non-teaching. It is true that there may be extraneous causes, such as undernourishment or mental defect, but these have long been noticed and taken account of.

For the normal and healthy, it is the very character of the school that seems to stop learning, and this at a point of no great difficulty: simple reading, writing, and arithmetic. The fifth grade is for many too many the stopping place. Is there a cause as yet unnamed? Some years ago a private group in New York invited public-spirited volunteers to teach reading to some youths in their late teens, dropouts from Harlem high schools. Results were uneven, disappointing. But one volunteer, a young publisher, told an inquiring reporter something revealing. After a couple of weeks of tutoring with no progress being made by any of the six big boys in his care, he decided to try meeting them one at a time, each day in the late afternoon. The response, one after the other, was unanimous: "Teacher, teacher, show me how to read!"

The desire, the "motivation" as jargon has it, was there, stifled by a state of mind which, if not created, had at least not been counteracted by the school itself. The unwritten law was: to show desire or ability to learn lowers one in the other fellows' regard. But the urge was there all along, nourished in secret and ready to burst out in private.

So taking as something native or family-inspired the resistance of the disadvantaged is a culpable error. A teacher must believe in the capacity of those he is teaching; it is defeatism to start out with the opposite assumption. If resistance continues, then the *students'* assumption that learning is below their dignity, sissified, must be met head on. The school must be assembled, the issue discussed, and consequences explained until the attitude is turned inside out and the deliberate non-learner ceases to be a hero for bucking the system.

This is where the role of the principal is decisive. Earlier, also in a Harlem school, a principal named Seymour Gang managed to bring the level of performance in all subjects well above the national average. That conspicuous example inspired a study by the Council for Basic Education. It found in different parts of the country four inner-city schools doing much better than the

rest, despite the supposed obstacle of an enrollment almost altogether "disadvantaged."* What made the difference was simple
enough: like Dr. Seymour Gang, the principal had a clear idea of
what he wanted to achieve, he chose and supervised his teachers,
helped and encouraged them to follow his lead. They came to
believe that reading, writing, and counting can be taught. With
everybody taking it for granted that learning is what is supposed
to go on in school, the pupils came to believe it too. Their pride
was in success, not sabotage; they were not bored enough to think
up mischief; there was rarely occasion for discipline.

But the bureaucracies did not like this report of the Council.
The principals themselves begged to have their names kept out of
the publication. They feared resentment and retaliation—some
merit-docking, which some indeed experienced. As for Seymour
Gang, not among those in the study, he was soon shelved by promotion and ultimately speeded out of the city system. Routines
must not be upset. Excellence is for sloganeering exclusively.

A more cheerful outcome rewarded another pioneer in the
same field, Twenty years ago, Mr. Blouke Carus, of the Open
Court Publishing Company near Chicago, finding that his young
children were not learning to read or write in the local public
school, diagnosed the trouble as the "look-and-say" method incar-
nated in Dick and Jane. He decided to launch a counter-offensive.
It was a vast undertaking: first, looking into the way phonics are
best taught, then devising and publishing textbooks and readers,
and finally training a sales force to teach teachers how to teach the
books. Meanwhile, the Reading Reform Foundation, founded in
1961, had been training or re-training teachers in the use of phonics. Both efforts have succeeded on a satisfactory scale, but there
are still large areas of the country in the grip of those who prefer,
day in and day out, to de-invent the alphabet.

Anyone who stops to think a moment can hardly help seeing
the rightness of the phonic mode of entry into the complexities of
the written word. It is precisely because the spelling of nearly all
languages is liable to many vagaries that mastery of the phonetic

* George Weber, *Inner-City School Children Can Be Taught To Read: Four Successful
Schools*, Council For Basic Education, Washington, D.C., 1971. The report made the
front page of the *New York Times*.

alphabet gives the comfort of a solid base for the mass of words that follow the rule. And the words that do not can at least be approximated. A simple anecdote makes the point: in the corridor of the elementary school the artwork of the first and second grades was posted—a vivid display of color and line. In the corner of one painting the viewer could read: *for mrs. Wilsn.* The young artist had had no occasion to see her teacher's name written, and under the regime of look-and-say she would never have had the remotest idea of its "look," for names would not be taught. But with sounded letters, all on her own, she was able to write her dedication unmistakably.

The lesson is plain. Children want to know how. Teaching helps to learn how when able people teach. But they must be allowed to do it, with guidance and encouragement as needed, and with the least amount of dictation from outside. Teaching is a demanding, often back-breaking job; it should not be done with the energy left over after meetings and pointless paperwork have drained hope and faith in the enterprise. Accountability, the latest cure in vogue, is to be looked for only in results. Good teaching is usually well-known to all concerned without questionnaires or approved lesson plans. The number of good teachers who are now shackled by bureaucratic obligations to superiors who know little or nothing about the classroom cannot even be guessed at. They deserve from an Education President an Emancipation Proclamation.

The gain would not be theirs alone. When good teachers perform and pupils learn, the sense of accomplishment produces a momentum that lightens the toil for both. Discipline is easier to maintain and failures become exceptions instead of the rule. As a further result there is no need for the fiddling and innovating, the "crash programs," all with more special funding and still more reports and evaluations and assessments. Since the millions go chiefly into new bureaus, new manuals full of "guidelines," and new textbooks that make only the publishers happy, the saving can be great. The taxpayers themselves benefit from a school that works.

In this description of what is possible, given the will, nothing utopian is supposed—or expected. But reform must bear directly on what is wanted, not try roundabout ways next door. The Army is not considered the most efficient of institutions, but when it finds a deficiency in fire power it does not launch a "Right to Shoot Program" or a "Marksmanship Recovery Project." It gets the sergeants busy and the instructors out to the rifle range.

The Centrality of Reading

. . . .

Queens College Conference on Reading, New York, 1969;
Michigan Quarterly Review, Winter 1970; *The Written
Word,* Newbury House, New York, 1971; *The Black Papers on
Education,* Davis-Poynter, London, 1971; *Books in Our Future,*
Library of Congress, Washington, 1987

A nybody who has ever taught knows that the act of teaching depends upon the teacher's instantaneous and intuitive vision of the pupil's mind as it gropes and fumbles to grasp a new idea.

This act of learning is surrounded by other acts less intense and perhaps also less productive. From the desk, the teacher gives instructions to the group, and not all the minds present attend to it with the same force, nor can the teacher square his or her mind with each of those other minds in perfect congruence.

Moreover, as in the jury scene of *Alice in Wonderland,* there are interruptions. The king having said, like a teacher: "This is very important," the White Rabbit interrupts: " 'Unimportant', your Majesty means." Just so will a child break in, from restlessness or too much zeal. All are affected: the jurymen write down "Important," "Unimportant," as chance dictates, that is, as their degree of concentration or self-assurance or feeling for one speaker or another leads them to do. That fictional scene is a brilliantly quick glimpse not of the courtroom alone, but also of the classroom.

A good teacher, of course, does not let himself be sidetracked or confused like the poor king, but he knows that in the instant of acquiring knowledge the mind is most vulnerable to distraction, and hence to error. Its antennae are vibrating fast, swaying and searching in all directions; the mind is conscious and unconscious at once in the most extraordinary way. The least atmospheric disturbance can deflect the perceiving power from the truth of the moment.

We can all remember early misconceptions which it took years to remove because they had taken root on some such occasion of king-and-rabbit vocal fluster. That is why oral teaching, indispensable to the close fitting of mind to mind, is also difficult, delicate, dangerous—and time-consuming. The state of congruence must be striven for over and over again about each aspect of the complex matters that form the branches of learning. Thanks to this repetition, there is opportunity to correct error, to refine the image of the worded idea, and most important, to establish habits of self-teaching—the habits we call reasoning, figuring out, catching one's mistakes before it is too late.

Now consider the only other situation in which learners also learn, the learning done from the written word. Here, if what is perceived is wrong, every repetition reenforces error. Here, if what is first perceived is confused, every repetition hardens confusion. A perpetual puzzle is as bad as a protracted error, and sometimes worse; for an error can be pulled up by the roots by main strength; whereas confusion needs long and hard work to turn into order.

There is therefore no excuse for allowing the exercise of reading to be less certain in its results then the exercise of listening and remembering. To tolerate reading that proceeds by guesswork, as if at a later time some one would surely tighten the screws of the loose mental structure and make it solid and precise, is to commit an injury against the growing mind. To allow the written word to be indefinite is to undo the incalculable technical advance that turned sounds into signs.

On this pedagogic ground alone, it could be said that no subject of study is more important than reading. In our civilization, at any rate, all the other intellectual powers depend upon it. No one can compute very far without reading correctly; no one can write decently without reading widely and well; no one can speak or listen intelligently without the mass of workaday information that comes chiefly through reading. As for acquiring some notions of history, government, hygiene, philosophy, art, religion, love-making, or the operation of a camera, they are all equally and pitifully dependent on reading. All the arguments against reading presuppose either a different culture, based on memory, myth, and physical prowess; or else a training in the interpretation of the purely visual which no one has ever begun to develop and which would doubtless require extra-sensory perception to make practicable.

Probably very few persons would systematically dispute these generalities. The most fanciful teachers, the laziest minds, acknowledge that several times a day they have to read the written word, if life—their life—is to go on; they are willing slaves to their own writings (a shopping list) or somebody else's ("Danger: live wire"). In the longer span, they cannot earn a living, choose a career, remember obligations, stay healthy, keep friends, and avoid jail without the aid of reading. It may be deplorable, but it is so. Imagine the art of reading lost—and with it writing, study, and verbal recovery—and it is hard to see how civilized man could survive the shocks and anxieties of his state, let alone serve his multitudinous desires.

We have only to recall what impediments wisdom runs into without the written word. The fifth-century Hindu philosophers who developed logic, ethics, and other means of sustaining mental balance depended entirely on memory for transmitting their achievements. "All this body of mental discipline," scholars tell us, "was taught without books. The style of the works themselves never lets us forget it, and they make shockingly bad *reading* in consequence. Often the only way to aid the burdened memory is an orderly but endless repetition of a verbal framework, wherein only one term of a series is varied at a time"—that is, one short sentence repeated with a change of only one word. "Yet the execution, in the absence of visible registering apparatus, [is] extraordinary. I am tempted to wonder how far the exaggeration of the Indian temperament and the temperateness of the Greek were

due to the absence and presence respectively, during the flores-
cence of each, of the fully written thought."*

The linguists who affect to scorn all utterance but the spoken
word, the teachers' group in the midwest that has discovered the
uselessness of reading and asks that it no longer be taught in the
schools, the zealots who sidestep the issue but sell futures in a
world where only the voice and the image will have currency—
all appear deficient in imagination, the imagination they would
need still more under their wayward scheme. In any case, their
prophecy of the end of reading leaves me unmoved, for prophecy
concerns the future, and to reach any future we must somehow
get from here to there, and that will require reading.

In such an itinerary, what is in fact the here from which we
start, the present situation of literacy? It is a state that does little
credit to our efforts. The universal light which, according to the
hopes of just a hundred years ago, when most of the great Education Acts were passed, was supposed to bathe the world in knowledge and reason, is not so dazzling as our generous ancestors expected. Its great source was to be literacy, and literacy is not in
the ascendant. There are in this country some twenty-five million
functional illiterates.** They are so-called because they cannot
function. We know also that among the latest adult generations
some two to three million such social cripples were discovered as
they came up for the draft.

These calamities are everybody's concern, but they can only
be repaired by teachers and other professionals adept at using the
right remedies. The professionals, in turn, need the backing of
parents, school boards, and interested by-standers. There must be
a public opinion in the question. *Where, in the matter of reading,
does the public interest lie?* Certainly, it is not the parents whom I
saw, in April, 1968, marching toward the Chicago City Hall to
protest against the lax promoting of their ill-prepared children,
who are abandoning the teaching of reading in favor of electronic
telepathy. These people know what they want for their children,
and they have a sound sense of what the country must require of

*Mrs. Rhys Davids, *Buddhism*, Home University Library, New York, 1911, p. 40.
**The count now, 20 years later, is 60 million (1990). (Ed.)

its future citizens. Only a sophisticated mind, that is, part-educated and full of unexamined ideas, could seriously advocate the carrying on of schoolwork without schoolbooks.

Where does that sophistication come from? Why did it seem plausible and attractive, after three thousand years of teaching reading by sounding each letter, to do just the opposite and encourage guesswork about the "shapes" of words? And now that this asinine substitution has massively failed as it deserved, why does it seem advanced and (once again) sophisticated to suggest that reading is after all expendable, since we have at command so many knobs and buttons with which to circulate counterfeits of visual and vocal reality?

The reason for the second of these frauds is made up of two parts. One is the desire to hide the original blunder, as the clumsy servant whisks out of sight the fragments of the broken cup. The other is simple blindness to the truth that reading and its necessary twin, writing, constitute not merely an ability but a power. I mean by the distinction that reading is not just a device (in jargon "a tool") by which we are reached and reach others for practical ends. It is also a mode of incarnating and shaping thought—as is implied in the example of the Hindu philosophers.

Now, all legitimate power is the result of a double discipline, first a discipline of the self and next a discipline of the acquired power. Concretely, in order to exert the power of reading, after disciplining eye, ear, and memory, one must at each word accept the discipline of the black marks on paper. Guessing and inferring by context, and forcing these dubious egotisms upon the written text, are a refusal to accept the symbolic constraints of the written word, after failing to constrain oneself to learn their clear demands.

Here we touch the political and social causes of the whole sad odyssey that has brought America to the condition of being, in the words of Arther Trace, "a land of semi-literates." The causes are not ignorance, poverty, or barbarous instincts; they are "advanced thinking," love of liberty, and the impulse to discover and innovate. It is from on top—by the action of the literate, the cultured, the philosophical, the artistic—that the common faith in the power of reading as central to western civilization has been destroyed. The target of the separate attacks and collective animus has been the very notion of power, discipline, and constraint.

For it is true that none of these looks like the rival goals that sophisticated thought preferred—the free play of fancy, creativeness, and immediate enjoyment; self-expression, novelty, and untrammeled choice in pursuing one's own thing. These pleasures have been touted in the writings of the best philosophers, artists, and political thinkers. And, with impatient contempt of school dullness and rote learning, educators resolved to emancipate the child and afford him these superior joys.

The folly consisted, not in wanting the lofty results, but in thinking that they could be reached directly. I have elsewhere defined this fallacy as "preposterism"—seeking to obtain straight off what can only be the fruit of some effort, putting the end before the beginning. It should have been obvious that self-expression is real only after the means to it have been acquired. Likewise, for the other pleasant exertions there are unavoidable conditions. These privileges of a free spirit are in fact exercised in meeting the conditions, in learning itself: the child *is* self-expressive when he painstakingly forms the letters *a, b, c*—though he is not quite ready to "create" a poem. Nor can creativeness be the *object* of his learning, since it is by definition unlearnable.

All this high-mindedness found expression in the look-and-say doctrine for the teaching of reading. The truth that practiced readers recognize whole words at a glance and do not need to sound each letter with their lips was pre-post-er-ously made the starting point of instruction—a method which on the face of it is the quintessence of anti-method. Thanks to flouting the alphabet the child was left free, imaginative, creative; the printed text exerted upon him no constraint whatever: he could not read. At the same time, the child was not free to start reading till some teacher decided that he was "ready"; was not free to read any book, least of all literature, but only Dick-and-Jane; was not free to connect his whole speaking vocabulary with what he was given to read, but only with 400, 500, 600 words, depending on his progress in guesswork; was not free to learn spelling at any decent rate, since a blank space has no "shape" and one cannot guess how to fill it without knowing the sounds of the letters. In the end, the desired "development of the self" did not seem to reach very far.

Whether this movement toward analphabetism can be reversed is what no one can predict. But before leaving the subject, it may be useful to mention the cultural forces that encouraged and still sustain the hostility to reading, to the alphabet, to the word.

The first is the emotion of scientism, which for seventy-five years has preferred numbers to words, doing to thinking, and experiment to tradition. This perversion of true science led to calling "experiment" almost any deviation from common ways of teaching. That it took half a century to begin admitting the error of look-and-say (through another "study," not through daily evidence of failure) shows the extent to which science has turned into superstition.*

Second, the last phase of the liberalism which by 1910 had proclaimed everybody's emancipation, including the child's, took the form of total egalitarianism. Everybody was, by democratic fiat, right and just in all his actions; he was doing the best he could; he was human: we knew this by his errors. It therefore became wrong to correct a child, to press him, push him, show him how to do better. Dialectal speech and grammatical blunders were natural and, as such, sacred; the linguists proved it by basing a profession on the dogma. Literature was a trivial surface phenomenon, the pastime of a doomed elite: why read books, why read, why teach the alphabet?

Third, the extension of free, public, compulsory education to all and in increasing amount (the high school dates from 1900) soon exhausted the natural supply of teachers. They had to be manufactured in large numbers, out of refractory material which could be more easily prepared in the virtues of the heart and the techniques of play than in any intellectual discipline. Themselves uneducated and often illiterate (see James Koerner's various reports),** they infallibly transmitted their inadequacies, turning

* See Jeanne Chall, *Learning to Read: The Great Debate,* New York, McGraw-Hill, 1967.

** James D. Koerner, *The Miseducation of American Teachers,* Little, Brown, Boston, 1963.

schoolwork into make-believe and boring their pupils into violence and scurrility.

Fourth and last, the conquest of the public imagination by
the arts, by "art as a way of life," has reinforced the natural resistance of the mind to ordinary logic, order, and precision—without
replacing these with any strong dose of artistic logic, order, and
precision. The arts have simply given universal warrant for the
offbeat, the unintelligible, the defiant without purpose. The
schools have soaked up this heady brew. Anything new, obscure,
implausible, self-willed is worth trying out, is an educational experiment. It has the aura of both science and art.

These contrasts do *not* mean that tradition is right and innovation wrong; that artists ought not to try making all things new;
that scientists may not experiment ad lib.; that the imagination
should not have free play; that equality is not the noblest of political ideas; that children should not be treated with courtesy and
affection. The point of the contrasts is this: what we have from
our expensive schooling is not what we thought we were getting.

What is the lesson to be drawn? It is that no principles, however true, are any good when they are misunderstood or stupidly
applied. Nothing is right by virtue of its origins, but only by virtue
of its results. A stifling tradition is bad and a "great" tradition is
good. Innovation that brings improvement is what we all desire;
innovation that impoverishes the mind and the chances of life is
damnable. Above all institutions, the school is designed for only
one thing—fruits. But nowadays we despise the very word cultivation. Unweeded soil undoubtedly grows wondrous things that
nobody can predict. Such things we have in abundance, but it
would be a rash man who would call it a harvest.

3

Middlemarch *Is*————?

(a military exercise—a Victorian novel—an English
holiday—March 15 at midnight)

INTRODUCTORY

Because the modern world lives by machine industry, it favors the
mechanical in all things, whether all things benefit from it or not.
We judge of the known and the unknown by numbers and make
do even with indirect clues to them—so-called indicators. We
choose employees by getting applicants to answer printed questions about their tastes, and we hope to cure mental illness by a
like survey of attitudes in imaginary scenarios. The answers are
totted up according to a code, and on the basis of it the hiring is
done or the prescription written.

That numerical remote control has invaded the school in the
form of multiple-choice tests, and their obvious convenience has
concealed a series of harmful side-effects. Those on the minds of
the learners and on the meaning of the things taught are detailed
in the essay that follows, but there are equally bad consequences
for other prime elements of schooling.

With printed tests, students do not write as often as they
once did. This self-evident remark holds the solution to the "writing problem" that schools vainly struggle with. Good writing,
done without groans at the injustice of the demand, comes only
with frequent practice. Short pieces must be called for regularly,
carefully corrected by the teacher, and rewritten until acceptable.
How often does that take place today? The answer is implied in
the announcement of yet another hopeful program offered at the
Bread Loaf School of English: "Making Johnny a Better Writer
By Getting Teachers to Write."

Essay examinations provide a second opportunity for writing, just as good readings provide the models. The printed test affords neither. Read the multiple-choice questions or the sentences to be dealt with in some prescribed way: their tone and shape are repetitious, colorless, uninspiring. Again, when it is so easy to "check off what's right," composition—the setting down of one word after another—comes to seem an unnecessary chore. This lazy view of writing begins in kindergarten with the "workbooks"—silly questions, ugly paper, crude pencilled checkmarks.

Older students who are not compelled to think up sentences of their own, who feel that the really serious problem is in which little box to put the *x,* never develop the habit of trimming and putting order among the ideas that come to their minds helter-skelter, in spurts, as ideas do to most people most of the time. Result: the inarticulate young whom one meets on every hand. Self-expression? They long for it, but too often it consists of fragments of thought jerked out with *like* and *y'know* as connectives and assembled for the listener only after several attempts.

It cannot be too often repeated that reading, writing, speaking, and thinking are not four distinct powers but four modes of one power. That last word is diagnostic: it means able to do at will. If instead of always using the jargon word "skills," school people used the word power, they might judge the result of their teaching more concretely. They would see that passing a fill-in test in English composition means nothing if the passer is power-*less*—not able—to write ten clear lines of prose. They would see further that something ought to be done for the student whose score on the test, again, was passing, but who cannot put together and utter the right words to make himself understood orally.

That is not the only complaint. Some students with a gift for writing are badly served too. They often find it difficult to do well on the fill-in writing tests, because their very ability to frame a sentence of their own runs counter to the trick of guessing what somebody else wrote in the printed test sentence that shows gaps within. A good writer is usually not one of those talkers who finish your sentence for you. His individuality is too strong and his mind too clear to himself to fall in with somebody else's intentions.

Finally, with scores in numbers comes the abdication of human judgment. It takes none to see that 520 is greater than 400. Very comforting. If the admissions officer follows his own impressions of the candidate he may make a mistake; with the score he is safe—safe in any later argument. Scholarship committees are notorious for this sort of cowardice: "Yes, I believe the recommendation, but the figures. . . ."

Does this mean that there should be no school grades? On the contrary. Letter grades are indispensable; they record a direct judgment by a human mind using a variety of evidences. They are not infallible, but they convey no fallacious exactitude; and when coming from several judges over a period of time they tend to balance and confirm each other. They are also much sounder than the verbiage of psychological descriptions and they distinguish degrees of merit far better than standardized scores.

Since these, as pointed out above, are an attempt to imitate the rigor of the machine, the topic next in order is the mechanized schoolroom. The push in that direction has been strong and persistent. Big business wants to sell the expensive machines developed for office use, and businessmen on schoolboards grasp the utility of these labor-saving devices better than they do the nature of teaching and learning. Thus in the sixties many came to think the "teaching machine" the cure-all. It would incite the young to teach themselves by giving answers to adroit questions on the screen and to learn their mistakes by its firm refusal to budge until the answer was right. Any coldness in this dreary intercourse was mitigated by flashed greetings and urgings of the friendliest kind. But drill without a drill-master is stupefying, and more interesting exercises were too difficult for most teachers to devise or administer. Most of the machines are now gathering dust in the basement storerooms.

Next came the audio-visual panoply of the seventies—the tape player and recorder, the slide-and-movie projector, the overhead reflector that threw on the screen whatever the teacher wrote or drew at his desk—quite "exciting" the first couple of days. All machinery is exciting when new; it soon loses its charm, for the mechanical does not stimulate thought, and as a wise man said: "Most important ideas aren't exciting. Most exciting ideas aren't important. Not every problem has a good solution." Of all the school gadgets, the film-strip projector is the chief survivor, and not because it teaches well, but because looking at a movie gives the class and the operator a break from real work.

The futility of these "aids" brings to memory the first of all the resorts to machinery: the typewriter—a special model for the small child. It was expected to relieve teacher and taught of the drudgery that goes with handwriting—so hard to teach, so dull to learn. Current commercial handwriting is a testimonial to the triumph achieved. Sizable losses in money, confusion and irritation in dealings are the product of, first, by-passing the human hand, and then refusing to restore the practice of loops and letters.

Today, the counterpart of the typewriter is the hand calculator, the substitute for arithmetic, and with it the introduction of the metric system. According to one of the many advocates of this joint improvement, "Such monstrosities as proper and improper fractions, numerators, least common denominators, and mixed numbers could be laid to rest." No doubt, and it would take a special talent to count a two-thirds majority of the Senate.

Next in line is the computer, whose applications are said to be endless. It is argued that since many children learn to use it at home to play games, it will be eagerly taken up at school. "Many" may be right, but surely not the children of poor parents, who are also many. This difference in home opportunity is doubly deplorable, being more crudely visible than any other, such as having books and parental help.

But that is not the only objection. First, a computerized classroom is very expensive; for a class of 25, it costs at present about $40,000. Money ought to go, now and in the future, to schoolteachers and school libraries. The computer, moreover, does not teach, does not show a human being thinking and meeting intellectual difficulties; it does not impart knowledge but turns up information pre-arranged and pre-cooked. For example, an actual demonstration of "referencing" shows the student encountering the name Mozart in the course of reading a story on the screen. By creating a "window" and without losing his story, he can summon up a portrait of the composer and a brief biography, while the opening bars of *Eine kleine Nachtmusik* resound through his earphones. Wonderful, isn't it? Wonderful for creating the cliché-ridden mind.

31

In other applications, such as spelling and grammar, the same rigidity obtains. The measure of good writing in the programs is sentence length. Only short sentences are deemed good, which is the negation of variety in prose and versatility in the writer. As for spell-check, it is a crutch that weakens the wish to know and can badly mislead, since it accepts any word correctly spelled, whether it is the intended word or not: if the subject is potatoes, *peal* is as good to the computer as *peel*.

So far, all the attempts at mechanization have failed—failed, that is, for the purposes of schooling. Industrial sales alone have benefited. Let us wish well to IBM and Macintosh and all their rivals, but urge that they keep out of the classroom. What goes on there should remain a live show.

Reasons to De-Test the Schools

Original Text Excerpted for Op-Ed Article in the *New York Times,* October 11, 1988

Many things have been urged upon the beleaguered public schools: install computers; reduce class size; pay teachers better and respect them more; give them bodyguards; reform teacher training; re-establish the principal's authority; create a rank of master teacher; let volunteers take on the chores; recruit liberal arts majors from the colleges; purge the bureaucracy and cut down paperwork; lengthen the school year; increase homework; stick to the basics; stop "social promotion;" set up remedial clinics; kill social studies and bring back history; wheel infants to the blackboard in their cradles; and—latest plan—pay the kids not to drop out or play truant.

Except for the last, these recommendations all have merit and some are being tried. But to the best of my knowledge, the central feature of modern schooling has never been singled out for critical discussion. I mean the use of multiple-choice tests.*

This type of test and its variants—filling in words, rearranging items, matching diagrams, choosing summary statements, and so on—dominates every mind in the classroom, the teacher's as well as the student's. Passing and failing, ratings of teachers and schools, national and state rankings, the rise and fall of literacy, admission to college and other institutions—all hang upon this instrument peculiar to our century.

I think its use harmful to teaching and learning, both. I know all the arguments in favor of these so-called objective tests. They are easy to grade. Uniformity and unmistakable answers secure fairness. With such tests one can compare performance over time and space and gauge the results of programs and devices. The questions and answers themselves are tested by the statistics of scores achieved and these again matched against later academic success.

If the tests do test what is supposed, these advantages look overwhelming and it must seem perverse to call the scheme harmful. But certainly, since its adoption the result of the huge outlay and effort of public schooling has been less and less satisfactory. The innumerable studies and reforms, federal reports and local anecdotes show failure on a scale way above the norm for human institutions. High school graduates cannot read or write acceptably, hardly know any history or geography, and are unable to cope with mathematics, science, and foreign languages.

What has this to do with mechanical testing? What does the practice contribute to the failure? Simply this: the device tests nothing but recognition knowledge. This is knowledge at the far side of the memory, where shapes are dim. Take a practical situation. A friend plans to drive to a town were you spent a month several years ago. Can you help him with some precise indications? Well, you remember a few landmarks—city hall, big church on main street, post office on one of the side roads. Your knowledge, distressingly vague, stops there.

* Since this article, debate has developed and the SAT has been revised, but mainly on the ground of unfairness to ethnic groups. (Ed.)

33

Yet if you join him and drive through that main street, it all comes back—things look familiar, including the names of shops and streets; you even notice changes. But—and this is the point— you did not *know* until you *saw.* You are glad to find that your memory is not a sieve, but when it was called on to perform without the renewed experience it was useless. It had only passive recognition-knowledge, not active usable-knowledge.

The application to schoolwork is obvious. Knowing something—really knowing it—means being able to summon it up out of the blue; the facts must be produced in their right relations and with their correct significance. When you know something, you can tell it to somebody else. It is these profound platitudes that condemn mechanical testing and its influence on the learning mind. Imagine the two different actions: it is one thing to pick out Valley Forge and not Albany or Little Rock as the place where Washington made his winter quarters; it is another, first, to think of Valley Forge and then to say why he chose it instead of Philadelphia, where it was warmer. (The pivotal fact here is that Philadelphia was in the hands of the British.)

In subjects that require something other than information, namely the development of skill, as in reading, writing, and arithmetic, the effort to find a plausible answer among the four choices vouchsafed from on high is even less instructional. Nobody ever learned to write better by filling in blanks with proffered verbs and adjectives. To write is to fill a totally blank sheet with words of your own.

Nor is this all. The tests, whether of fact or skill, confuse the mind by thrusting into it irrelevant ideas—and why four, not three or five? With any number must come perpetual doubts, which is not the right mood for showing what one knows. The doubts are reinforced by the wording of the questions. They must be scanned in lawyer-like fashion, because by their nature they cannot be framed in a simple, candid way, like essay questions; they are catch questions.

The worst feature of this game of choosing the ready-made instead of producing the fresh idea is that it breaks up the unity of what has been learned and isolates the pieces. In going through the 50 or 100 questions nothing follows on anything else. It is the negation of the normal pattern-making of the mind. True testing issues a call for patterns, and this is the virtue of the essay examination. Both preparing for it and taking it reinforce the pattern originally formed, and degrees of ability show themselves not in the number of lucky hits, but in the scope, coherence, and verbal accuracy of each whole answer.

Science and mathematics consist of similar clusters of truths; in every subject, to show a grasp of any portion means making organized statements or constructing logical demonstrations, and to do this calls for full-blown thinking. Objective tests ask only for sorting. What has been the upshot of glorifying that particular exercise? Many teachers, entire schools, schedule practice sessions in test-taking to get more students through. Then, finding that the victims are cripples in consecutive thought, they set up "courses in thinking." As if thinking could be taught apart from the subject-matter—the subjects already in the curriculum, now fragmented by the multiple-choice tests.

Of course, teachers in most schools today would be appalled at the idea of giving only, or mainly, essay examinations. Large classes and the load of extraneous paperwork make it impossible to read *and correct* several batches of papers each time a test is appropriate. This obstacle cannot, indeed, be got over. But what it means is not that objective tests are good; it means that present school arrangements are bad. Judge by comparison: a good hospital is one where physicians have the skill, the time, and the equipment to give patients adequate care. Any scamping, all short cuts are excusable only during emergencies, after some great disaster. From which it follows that schools, which shortcut an important function of teaching, have been run for decades on a disaster basis, a perpetual emergency.

Essay examinations do not help only the learner but also the teacher, for only by reading what the pupil says can the teacher get to know the individual young mind and intelligently help its development. This one needs to sharpen thought and expression, that one needs loosening up in feeling and imagination, a third must acquire a better sense of fact.

The truth is, when all is said and done, one does not *teach a subject,* one teaches a student how to learn it. Teaching may look

35

like administering a dose, but even a dose must be worked on by the body if it is to cure. Each individual must cure his or her own ignorance. Accordingly, all sound educational theory enjoins individual attention. But where is the individual in a numerical score?

Can nothing be said, then, in favor of multiple-choice as indicators of some part of school performance? Yes, they are serviceable and convenient as quizzes. When the teacher wants to know whether some reading assignment has been done, a mechanical test of any sort—true-false, multiple choice, or the simple identification of names and terms—gives an indication; and the knowledge that such a test will be given also inspires the eager and rouses the laggards. But passing this exercise gives no measure of the student's understanding, only of his recent memory, and the test should count for little if anything in the final grade.

To bring back essay examinations would call for reviving the lost art of framing and grading questions. Every question ought to elicit knowledge of a unified portion of the subject covered and bring out what the teaching has aimed at over and above the factual underpinnings. To frame such questions and make them fair, precise, fully relevant is not an art the unpracticed teacher can improvise. Good teachers *learn* how to compose an examination by recalling their own best experience in college and by consulting and imitating their elders in the department.

These same aspects of question-making enter into the case against multiple-choice testing. Thirty years ago, the late physicist and mathematician, Banesh Hoffmann, wrote a book entitled *The Tyranny of Testing,** which was attacked by the test-making industry and ignored by the educationists. What it showed by examples over a wide range of subjects was how the multiple-choice questions in use, by their form and contents, worked against the aims of good teaching. Leaving to one side the errors of fact and misleading wordings that he came across in sample tests, he found that this mode of testing suppresses the natural diversity of minds, penalizes the more imaginative, and perpetuates conventional

---

*Crowell-Collier, New York, 1962; Foreword by Jacques Barzun.

opinions. The students who handle multiple choices best are not the best, but the second-best.

It follows that the many kinds of test scores that the nation relies on for a great many decisions about individuals, young and old, mislead the users. Some college admission officers have by now gone so far as to say that the dreaded Student Aptitude Test (SAT)—that rite of passage which the young not only cannot escape, but which they must go through more than once—is "no better" than the high school record as a predictor of success.

This is progress, but not enough. The country is still enslaved to the practice of pushing and coaching the young in the art of how to pass with scatter-knowledge. Parents, administrators, pundits, and editorialists judging schools, teachers, systems, and students are still content to substitute the mark of an indefinite performance for the assessment of genuine ability.

In matters of learning and teaching that assessment can only be done, however fallibly on occasion, by competent minds examining directly the work of other, prentice minds. Instead of forcing these last (some still in kindergarten) to concentrate their lives on endless form-filling exercises till it seems natural to equate knowledge with "Take a chance and choose," the schools would be well advised to stop and heed Emerson's advice: "Tell us what you know."

4

Textbook Into Scrapbook

INTRODUCTORY

The next essay describes a feature of modern schoolwork that has gone largely unnoticed. It is the character ("but not what you think") of the television programs children see in the home. Therefore, although parental oversight is briefly referred to, it is not discussed. Here, however, the relation of parent, child, and school claims attention.

The latest cry in the clamor for reform is, "Get the parents involved!" One would suppose that having a child in school would mean involvement, automatically. But the new demand proposes to let, or make, the parents take part in guiding, monitoring, and even choosing their children's school. Are they capable of it? On what basis and with what ends in view?

The first notion that comes to mind is that parents are already running things through school boards—16,000 of them—and though exceptional ones exist (there are important exceptions to every generality), it is obvious that most boards have done a poor job of management. They have chosen the superintendents, backed their plans and appointments, spent money for endless innovations, and they have done this for forty years before seeing the oncoming disaster. Even now they see the failure but not the errors. What likelihood is there that bringing in more parents, all parents, as part-time school governors would produce saner results?

To begin with, not all parents see the school *or their children* in the same way. Some are concerned with steady progress, with grades, with homework, which they want to see done; they visit the teacher and learn how they may assist instruction. Others are indifferent and some hostile; they want their children to get through well enough, but they take a scornful view of what is taught (often rightly, as it happens); they resent bad marks or classroom reproof, and they go to the school only to abuse those they hold responsible. Nor have all these critics the education to encourage or supplement at home what the school is managing to impart.

It is this mixed constituency that is now looked to as savior. But how to organize salvation? There are already parent-teacher associations that do good work, though many are balked by the impenetrable jargon of the educational authorities. The laity can only listen, get a dim notion, and approve—as if there should be a laity with regard to the words used about schooling. Everything should be clear as day in an institution whose object is to bring light.

Going beyond parent-teacher associations would mean some form of local "town meeting," giving everybody a voice while teachers and principals listen and heed. Or if too cumbrous, then a representative body elected by the community to make known its wishes and suggestions, and this body too would be subdivided into committees to deal with the different parts and needs of the institution. These schemes have only to be stated to show their unpracticality. A school can no more be run by committees and votes than can a ship.

The parental legislature would be Babel and the school people would go mad. They are already beset by inhuman demands and impossible directives; the additional nonsense they would hear would defy assimilation, even though much of it would simply echo the daily verbiage of the educationists.

These same parents are also threatened with the task of choosing their child's school by means of the voucher system. The voucher represents the sum of money currently spent on each child's public schooling. With this money order in hand, the parent goes in any one year to school A or B or C, thus creating by competition a free market productive of better schools. Such is the theory.

One wonders where the advocates of the plan have stored

their imagination. Visualize the school and its personnel which, for some reason, good or bad, have fallen in popular esteem. How soon do they hear that next autumn there will be only a trickle of students, children of the uninformed? What is then done with teachers and principal, librarian and janitors, books and supplies ordered and delivered?

Again, on what basis do the parents judge? Gossip at first, no doubt. But soon there will be a little industry publishing guides. These will be based on "scores" of various kinds, including polls of the local parents, and such things as the number of books in the library and of film projectors in the classrooms. It will be another Grand Abstraction masquerading as a competent judgment.

Costs will go up, necessarily. For one thing, the wandering scholars aged six to sixteen will have to be taken by bus from home to distant school if that should prove the theoretical best. That school will need extra funds for additional staff to handle the sudden flood and perhaps for renting an annex if space is short. At the same time, of course, the teachers defeated in the popularity contest will have to receive compensation or severance pay. Their union will rightly see to that.

Now it is more than likely that the country as a whole spends enough money right now to support an adequate public school system. The money is not equitably distributed everywhere, because most of it is raised from local taxes in counties differing in wealth. But that imbalance is being gradually corrected. It is the funding of irrelevant, utopian, or counter-productive purposes that brings on the demand for ever more support. Special schools (e.g. "magnet," "alternative"), opulent athletics, pilot projects, remedial work, all generate great expense—administrators, offices, filing cabinets, mimeographed paper. Private schools, and especially parochial ones, are run on administrative budgets far leaner than those of public schools. Estimates vary from one-fifth to one-quarter the cost. If we add to the current public expense the predictable costs of the voucher system, a great infusion of new money will really be needed.

These inflationary ways of managing schools and these attitudes about them are among the outside forces that interfere with success; the inside forces are no less powerful, and they derive from the same habits of mind and behavior. If, as estimated, many children spend thirty hours a week in front of the screen and neglect homework (supposing they are given any), it is because parents are indifferent or feel powerless, but also because they have no clear idea of what a school can and should do. They are, after all, the products of that same, ineffectual, incoherent schooling.

Television and the Child
—But Not What You Think

. . . .

The Folger Library, Washington, D.C., November 17,
1986; *Basic Education*, Fall 1987

The title of my remarks refers to a familiar question: is television harming children in their schooling? The answer is obviously yes if the screen keeps children from doing homework. But so would any other abuse of working time—playing in the yard or reading comic books. All these are questions for parents. The deeper question is whether television *by its nature* disables learning.

It looks to me as if it did, because its formula is: Discontinuity. An expert has said that the image on the screen must change every 18 seconds, if not sooner. Indeed, the "sound bite"—uninterrupted speech—has gone down from 42.3 seconds in 1968 to 9.8 seconds in 1987. Program directors and producers, I am told, think according to a "doctrine of moments." We might ask, what makes them act this way? In answer I would venture the paradox that our jittery television is as it is because of influence from the schools.

This influence has been both direct and indirect. The direct influence is that the men and women who work in television are products of the schools and what they produce shows how their minds work. The indirect influence is that of the audience. They too have come out of the common school, and if they get bored regularly at 17 ½ seconds, they are no doubt reproducing the character of their schooling.

What entitles me to say this? Simply that during the last 50 years, nearly everything done in school has tended toward the discontinuous, the incoherent, the jiggly.

Have you ever looked into a modern textbook—say in American history for the 8th grade? Its closest analog is a travel brochure. On a double-page spread in four colors, you see a small map, a picture of Benjamin Franklin, a set of dates and figures framed in black lines, a Wigwam, a view of Philadelphia in the 18th century, a list of questions off in a corner. The design is visually stunning, obviously done by an expert in display advertising. Among these eye-catching items, there is a thin stream of print meandering diagonally from left to right. It probably says something, though its position does not invite reading. But in the list of questions the first is really interesting. It asks: How old do you think B. Franklin was when this engraving was made?

If you do read the text, shutting your mind to the colorful layout, you find that it tries to teach the pupil every kind of history—a jumble of political, social, economic, and cultural fact and opinion. It also tries to teach tolerance, compassion, and global understanding, inevitably at the expense of pursuing one line of thought. Its principle is: bits and pieces. It reminds one of the TV commercial, the preview of the film, the broken-up talk show, the scatter-shot news report.

Such a textbook typifies the attitude of the school toward the mind of the learner at any age. The pupil must be continually lured by bright externals, and during distraction, fed in small mouthfuls. Nothing must last long, nothing must look systematic. The conclusion seems compelling: television programs are put together *by* the products of our schools *for* the products of our schools. Remember that television came later than the modern school.

The next question is: how did the schools get that way? Well, there was the desire to make schooling less stuffy than before, to bring it closer to life. Life is always a medley; it is fragmented, jerky, often colorful—so let the class take up things the way they look in life. No more memorizing and reciting, no more reading full pages of print and writing essays—break up all this sitting and listening for one continuous period to the teacher and the other pupils. Instead, let's have individual projects, field trips and filmstrips—abolish monotony. Let the class decide what it does next. Remove the desks and seats, put carpeting down, and let us read and write in Nature's way—on the floor, squatting or stretched out, chattering about the world. Teacher is there to orchestrate these lifelike activities.

A second influence has been science. I mean science as a cultural force. It suggested that the old ways of teaching, being pre-scientific, must be wrong. New and correct methods would be found by educational research and the findings of child psychology. Experiment and watch improvements accrue. You could then predict and guarantee results.

Pressure from science and from life joined behind innovation, though their principles were opposed. Science said, "Never mind common sense, research always brings out surprising novelties worth trying." But these run counter to practical experience, and the result was that schoolwork became more and more like try-outs for new shows, and less and less successful when tested by ordinary standards, such as: can they read? can they count?

Where the two forces were at one was in a common assumption as to what knowledge is and how to detect its presence. Beginning with the small child's workbook, what is expected is the rapid filling-in of blanks hinting at disconnected items of information. Success in school consists in learning to deal with the printed forms that future life holds in store. It is odd that in an age when the word context is continually used as a reminder of the way things hang together, people should have tolerated schools where context is hourly destroyed.

With the American love of bandwagons, educational schemes sweep the country and establish in the school mind only one habit: that self-same habit of discontinuity. Programs, courses, and "objectives" are intellectual transients; and that cast of mind is inevitably transmitted to the learning child.

Science also introduced into teaching the virus of explicit

psychology. It too was lifelike. For as we all know from person-
ality testing and amateur psychologizing, the various brands of
the science pervade business, employment, religion, marriage,
the criminal law, friendship, and biography. In the schools, psychology has tended to substitute therapy for teaching and made
the explanation of failure more important than its correction. Indeed, it has even disallowed correction as humiliating.

Meanwhile, it petrified the parents through report cards in jargon
that was incomprehensible because meaningless. Worst of all, it
committed the grave fault of making children self-conscious. One
of the virtues of learning anything is that it takes one out of oneself and into a subject—something independent existing out
there, in the world of fact or ideas, or both. To pull the mind back
into self-concern and self-excuse is not only a hindrance to learning, it is also a deprivation of the feeling of community with others. A subject understood in common with other people is a social
bond, and of a kind most desirable in a democracy. So again, by
separating little egos and by taking attention away from the subject to the self, one more agent of discontinuity was introduced
into the classroom. It was morally culpable besides, for children
as they grow up have enough internal causes of self-consciousness
and enough difficulty in coping with it.

Finally, the curriculum itself has been inspired by discontinuity. To begin with, too many subjects of study attempted and the
basic subjects themselves turned into exercises in scrappiness.
The prototype is the well-known hash called social studies, its
counterpart being the course in general science.

Part of the motive behind these catchall courses is to cover
a lot of ground, but another part is indulgence for restlessness.
The principle of "keep them excited" is thought to be the only
answer to boredom. But it is a great mistake to implant the idea
that learning can be steadily exciting, or that excitement is a good
frame of mind for acquiring knowledge. Developing a genuine
interest in a subject comes only after some drudgery, and only
when the learner gets to the point of seeing its order and continuity, not its intermittent peaks of excitement.

The same objection applies to the way in which school programs have been administered. What is offered has long since ceased to be a curriculum; it is a collection of interchangeable units (often called modules), which represent not just subjects but also periods of time, some as short as 25 minutes. The goal is "flexibility"—meaning that in high school it is frequently the students themselves who make up programs of long and short modules to fit taste and convenience. For this purpose, the catalogue is a thick book that describes the offerings with great candor, the courses for dedicated students being paired with others certified not to lie so heavy on the stomach.

Given this haphazard manner of developing the young mind, it is comforting to remember that the school provides other things besides teaching. Athletics and extra-curricular activities and numerous groupings and gatherings fill in the gaps between the atomized courses and offer the students a few forms of consecutive experience during which they cannot help learning something. Ten years ago, an educational official in Washington estimated that the amount of time the public schools devoted to academic work was 18%.

It is not hard to imagine what the mind of an average boy or girl contains after 12 years of modules, Dick and Jane, film strips, social studies, grade B electives, and "research" for acting out the surrender at Appomattox. Some information has undoubtedly stuck, thanks to a good teacher, or a self-developed interest in a subject or hobby such as photography or computer manipulation. But anything like a reasonable grasp of any fundamental subject should not be looked for. It would be unjust to these normally bright and inquisitive young people to expect from them what they have been denied.

The worse of it is that they have been left without the means to help themselves. Many cannot read or understand what they do read. A high school teacher in the Northwest coped with that difficulty by having the majors in theatre make tapes of her assignments in history and then sent her classes to listen to the tapes.

Now what is the antidote? How should knowledge be administered, not at a distance by officialdom, but inside the classroom? The need for unity and continuity in thought and subject should be matched by unity and continuity in work. The length of a period of instruction should of course be proportioned to the age of the child, but it should be long enough to make concentration and absorption progressively easier. This implies other things— desks and chairs, no reading or research on the floor, no running about. The whole class should attend to the same thing, so that it may learn not only from the teacher but from its own members' errors and successes. It is better that the boy in the back row should throw an occasional spitball than that all 30 pupils should continually dash about on separate projects.

The permanent aim should be to increase the span of attention. It can be done. An interesting proof came not long ago from a review of an English-television comedy-program for children. The reviewer expressed surprise that "unlike much American comedy, the imported shows don't assume a short attention span." English schooling has deteriorated like ours, but apparently not as far, since English children can take more than 18 seconds of slapstick and gags without feeling their minds going blank.

One thing that formal psychology can tell the teacher is that attention comes in beats, in waves. Good teaching therefore strives to connect these beats into a steady rhythm; it revives interest by variety, emphasis, relevant surprise—just as good writing does. But obviously, nothing is accomplished if variety is merely change of occupation. The change must occur within the subject, it must be about the same purpose—until the pupil develops the ability to keep going by himself. That is what learning to study means.

Right now, in despair, some schools are "experimenting" with courses in problem-solving and in critical thinking. The school has not taught how to learn; now it wants to climb that Mt. Everest of intellect, critical thought. Critical thinking can only be learned by the discussion of an idea which is part of a subject, under the guidance of an able thinker. Thinking is like piano-playing; it is shown, not taught.

And in this new effort, the school is repeating one of its old mistakes, which I am sorry to say was originally due to John Dewey. Dewey is often made responsible for all the errors and follies of the so-called "progressive school" of the 1920s. This total blame is unjust. He never intended that schoolwork should be the same as play; he did not subordinate intellect to moral attitudes; and he did not advocate the à la carte curriculum. Only one item in his program—and in his philosophy—was wrong. This was his belief that all thinking is problem-solving. In his influential little book *How We Think,* he described the five steps by which the mind solves a problem. The thinker meets a difficulty, defines it, makes a hypothesis, gathers facts, and verifies—or disproves—the hypothesis. But this pattern does not even apply to the way scientific solutions are found, only to the way they are written up. A good many scientists and mathematicians have told us how they struggle with problems; their ways are not alike, and they rarely follow Dewey's steps, like a marcher in a parade. Quite often, it is the unconscious mind that pops out a solution after sleeping on the problem.

What is even more important, the greater part of thought does not deal with problems. We have all got into the habit of calling every purpose or difficulty a problem, to the point where some people on hearing "Thank you" no longer say "You're welcome;" they say "No problem." A problem is a definable difficulty; it falls within certain limits and the right answer gets rid of it. But the difficulty—not the problem—the difficulty of making a living, finding a mate, keeping a friend who has a jealous, cantankerous disposition cannot be dealt with in the same way—it has no solution. It calls for endless improvisation, some would say "creativity." So we come to the conclusion that the mind at its best thinks not like Dewey's imaginary scientist, but like an artist. Art is achieved not by problem-solving but by invention, trial and error, and compromise among desired ends—just like good government. We may thereby gauge how far from practical is the opinion that if we teach problem-solving, or critical thinking, we shall equip young minds for dealing with all of life's predicaments.

By this foray into Thinking, we have come back to psychology, which I have said has little or nothing to offer the teacher. A true science delivers only general truths and statistical probabilities, and there is no such thing as *the* child. Each individual is different and does not act as the book says he will at this age or that. Indeed, a child does not even stay of the same mental age from day to day. If a teacher works according to the rule, instead of observing and instinctively adapting means and ways to the live situation, he or she is in the wrong profession. Any true teacher knows that one must often do the very opposite of the usual or the recommended. One has the care of a particular mind, not of a type.

In other words, the teacher must be, not a psychologist or scientist, but a politician or statesman, a diplomat, an artist. The art is that of understanding and persuasion, so as to carry the listener toward the same understanding. This is done by constant awareness of other persons and instant response to their concerns—all this without losing sight of the goal to be achieved. It is a demanding task, which is why there are relatively few born teachers.

In his delightful book *Talks to Teachers,* William James, himself a master psychologist, expresses his belief that a knowledge of "the ordinary workings of the mind" is enough for the teacher. He adds that "the vital thing about the pupil, his emotional and moral energy, becomes known only by the total results in the long run." He also makes it clear that there is no possibility of making schoolwork always easy and "natural." Much of it is hard and *un*natural until it has become a habit. Effort is always needed, and the utmost the teacher can do to supply interest is "to let loose the effort."

If we must have slogans for schools, "let loose the effort" strikes me as the one to adopt. The young in this country are uncommonly intelligent and vigorous. They are worldly beyond their years, thanks perhaps to television and the new ways of parenthood. Their energies outside the classroom are certainly impressive, including their harmful energies. If schoolwork were restored so as to recapture their minds, with teachers teaching instead of innovating and distracting, the results might well seem miraculous. These conditions may sound hard to regain after so many years of folly and failure, but unless they are met, not with theory but in practice, we cannot hope to let loose the effort.

5

Ideas versus *Notions*

The word nonsense in the next section is not an insult but a description. In the last fifty years, so many school methods, plans, programs, innovations, and "experiments" have failed that they must be accounted lacking in sense, in good sense. That conclusion was implied in a recent headline: "School Reform Again—Sigh".

But the pressing need will not go away with sighing, and experience suggests that before trying once more to make schools function properly, one thing ought to become clear—the source of the nonsense, so as to avoid another round of the absurd. Many observers have blamed "the progressive school" and its putative father John Dewey. Others have found the trouble to be obsolete equipment and unbusinesslike management. Buy audio, radio, video, reprographo devices, on the one hand; and on the other, subsidize research into new methods, new ways to motivate and teach. Then use the plant all year round, set up internal audit, and give bonuses for productivity.

Dewey and progressivism, glanced at earlier, are dealt with in what follows this note. The other proposal, with its zeal for making things hum, has up to now been adopted piecemeal. It too breeds nonsense, because it ignores the nature of teaching and the purpose of a school. In fact, educational nonsense always comes from zeal displacing soberness and flouting the conditions of the two fundamentals: teaching and learning.

To be a school means to teach some few well-known things, for only certain things can be taught, as will be indicated in a moment. What needs attention first is the host of the non-

teachable that have made the modern school scamp its duty and
fail.

Some years ago, a new school superintendent in the South-
west calculated that by state authority he must find room in the
high school curriculum for about 200 subjects. They included:
driver education, sex education, kindness to animals, shopping
and local resources, care for endangered species, family living,
global understanding, and *no* sex education. Legislatures are ever
ready to add requirements that sound worthy or useful. Few survive in practice, but enough are attempted to make a mockery of
the idea of schooling.

The head of the National Education Association, true to its
baneful tradition, has said that "teachers must be social workers,
psychologists, priests"—three professions for the price of one,
and without benefit of seminary or graduate training. It would be
seen as quackery if the stubborn will of the educationists and the
foolish hope of the public had not accustomed everybody to the
imposture. "The School Must Also Teach an End to Hate" is
the plea of an anguished citizen. "Environmental Education,"
proposes a retired professor of education. As long as these ideas
are considered tenable, schoolwork properly so called remains an
underground activity in a tyrannical regime.

Schools are not intended to moralize a wicked world but to
impart knowledge and develop intelligence, with only two social
aims in mind: prepare to take on one's share in the world's work
and, perhaps in addition, lend a hand in improving society, *after*
schooling is done. Anything else is the nonsense we have been
living with.

Hence the school authority's first duty is to settle the question, Is it teachable? Take "family living." Can it be organized as
a subject? The facts of family life, if reliable, are a mass of statistics that change every year; the rest is advice about behavior. Neither can be reduced to rules. There is nothing solid to remember
and apply systematically. So this very important segment of life
cannot be "a subject."

All that such Good-Samaritan courses amount to is pieties.
They present moralizing mixed with anecdotes, examples of good
and bad, discussions of that catchall word "values," and they

punctuate the random talk with "research" and play-acting by the students—wholesale make-believe. And dangerous, too: the best and the worst students alike are bored. They know they are not gaining any new powers. Nor do they relish continual preachiness any better than adults.

Are we to conclude that a proper school can do nothing to foster ethical behavior? Of course it can—by being a well-run school in the full meaning of the term. Ethics must be seen to be believed, and school life is full of situations in which decent, generous, even noble actions can take place and be known to all so as to be felt as *the right thing to do*. Ethics is not talk but action.

One great source of nonsense, then, is trying to teach the virtues verbally. A second is engineering human traits. The aim is to reach certain results head on. For example, it is true that students are hampered if they think poorly of themselves; they need a certain amount of self-esteem. Why not *give* it to them? Eighty-three percent of teachers in a recent inquiry considered this their "top role." Two states have added to their education departments a "Bureau of Self-Esteem." All this as if self-esteem were a definite commodity that one has or hasn't and that can be produced and injected when lacking.

What a bureau can certainly produce is more bureaucracy, with paperwork and jargon to burden and bewilder teachers still more. Self-esteem comes from work done, from new power over difficulty, which in school means knowing more and more and coping easily with serious tasks. Boredom disappears with progress, with perceived advance toward completion and mastery.

Just as it is foolish to go scheming for more self-esteem, so it is to expect a course to pump up intelligence, like oil, to the surface of the mind. This is attempted, for example, in courses where the young "learn to analyze the news." History well-taught would enable a graduate to do just that forever after, instead of tying him down to some particular technique devised by a textbook writer and imposed for a semester on the local newspaper.

A sure sign of nonsense in the offing is the emergence of new names for well-known things. Under the educationist regime English became "language arts;" the school library, "general information resource;" the school period a "module." A while ago, a large western city set up "literacy centers" in its branch libraries, meaning remedial courses. Notice: the new term is always vaguer than the old, making the results of the novelty harder to judge, and the work is moved to a "center," as if success would be easier in a new suit of clothes. Why should literacy be fostered elsewhere than in a school? Perhaps the school, fully occupied by nonsense, has no room for literacy.

At any rate, now that everybody knows the condition of the school system and there is talk of a national core curriculum, thinking about the teachable, the possible, can no longer be evaded. What is a school subject? First come the means of further learning, which are reading, writing, and counting. It was their barefaced neglect that made a small group of people in the 1950s form the Council for Basic Education, which in turn led to the popular formula of "Back to the basics."

But the Council never thought that the three R's were enough, and it argued for a return to the long-tried curriculum of History, English and Foreign Languages, Science, Mathematics, and the Arts, including Literature. Their first common characteristic is that they are known to have been taught successfully, in this country and elsewhere, for generations. The second explains why they are teachable. It is that their facts can be organized; rules and principles can be derived to make their study systematic and progressive: one year's work follows another rationally, even though at some points convention enters into the linking.

Such are the ways in which a subject, meaning a school subject, differs from a topic. Hundreds of topics are interesting and important, but they cannot be made scholastic for lack of these features. In the topic Local Resources, for instance, a mass of facts can be pulled together about public transportation, the police and fire departments, the welfare administration, the bureaus of parks, recreation, and marriage licenses, the office of consumer affairs, the garbage collecting, the schools and hospitals, and no doubt a dozen other services. But nothing leads from one to the other, except the individual inhabitant who may need them, and no rules or principles emerge from surveying the lot. Supposing a year devoted to describing this civic offering in some detail, what would be left in the mind would be a haphazard collection of items, different in each student mind according to chance or special interest. What would have been carried out is not an idea but a mere notion.

Where the Educational Nonsense Comes From

. . . .

Open Court Editorial Board, June 7, 1971;
Papers on Educational Reform, vol. II, 1971; *Intellectual Digest,* October 1971; Pembroke College, Cambridge University, January 1, 1972; *Conference,* Norwich (Eng.), February, 1972; *The Basic Unity of Education,* National Council for Educational Standards, London, 1972

T he first thing we must know under this heading of educational nonsense is where it does *not* come from. But before we can clear the ground, obviously we must agree about what we mean by nonsense. For the present purpose I call nonsense any plan or proposal *or critique* which plainly disregards the known limits of schooling or teaching. Schooling means teaching in groups. Thus a plan that might be workable if applied by a gifted tutor to a single child living continuously in the same house becomes nonsense when proposed for classroom instruction in an institution designed for hundreds or a national system designed for millions.

Similarly, the limits of teaching are transgressed if the plan presupposes extraordinary talents or devotion in the teacher. Finally, nonsense is at the heart of those proposals that would replace definable subject matters with vague activities copied from "life" or with courses organized around "problems" or "attitudes." The attempt to inculcate directly, as a subject of instruction, any set of personal, social, or political virtues is either indoctrination or foolery. In both cases it is something other than schooling. That fact is not in conflict with another fact, which is that schools indirectly impart principles of conduct. Schools reinforce some portion of the current ethos, if only because teachers and books and the normal behavior of those brought together exemplify the moral habits of the time and place.

Summing up, we may say that educational nonsense consists in proposing or promoting something other than the prime object of the school, which is the removal of ignorance. Or again, it consists in undertaking to do what cannot be done within the conditions of time and talent set by the common realities of life. Applying these standards, we can perhaps see where the current supply of educational nonsense does *not* come from.

It does not come from the quite imaginary storehouse of folly called Romanticism. It does not come from the writings of Rousseau or the teachings of William James or John Dewey. This is not to say that the purveyors of contemporary nonsense do not invoke those authorities and precedents, or that they do not borrow from the men and the movement I have cited. But these borrowings are trivial or mistaken and prove nothing; if we do not want to engage in nonsense ourselves, we must refrain from attributing the vulgar errors of today to thinkers beside whom our would-be theorists are but broken echoes.

To begin with, Romanticism is a movement of ideas of which pedagogical doctrines form only a small part. What the movement as a whole tried to ascertain and establish was the role of impulse, feeling, and will in the work of the mind. And as to this fundamental link, we are all strictly "romantics;" it is therefore silly to use that name as a term of abuse. We accept, for example, the "romantic idea" that individuals are in part unique, that this fact produces among pupils a diversity of talent, interest, and rate of development, and that both individuality and diversity are desirable.

It was the early romantic Rousseau who said how important for teaching was the *activity* of the mind; but in his tract on education he tried to show something more—to point to new goals for education, and thus to condemn the old. Why was this substitution necessary? The answer is simple enough and it never varies with time or place. The perpetual task of the educational reformer is to say: "Look! Whatever your good intention was fifty years

54

ago, it has now hardened into a deadly, oppressive, meaningless routine. Since you are not likely to recapture the freshness of the former effort, let me urge a new effort, with the observable child as its starting point."

The recurrent hardening of the arteries and this periodic denunciation of it explain why, for instance, learning poetry by heart is suddenly deemed wicked; why lecture courses become an abomination; why diagramming sentences is assailed as a violation of human rights. Someone discovers, quite simply, that the point of doing these things has been lost. Originally they were sensible devices; now they are administered in a dull mechanical way, because the teacher has lost the sense of their novelty and difficulty. Few things retain their significance when they are done without difficulty or at least a dash of *in*experience.

The historic reformers of education share another significant trait: nearly all consciously propose ideal models. They draw a perfect circle, knowing full well that any school, any form of teaching must remain a crude polygon. Yet an alert teacher can make headway along the new direction they indicate. For they also describe a desirable frame of mind—the opposite in all ways of the mindless stagnation visible in whatever schools they observe.

The curious thing is that the new direction and frame of mind are repeatedly the same at each reform: the direction is always toward concrete reality, the world of things, the spontaneity dimmed by convention. Read Rabelais, Montaigne, Comenius, Aubrey, Locke, Rousseau, Pestalozzi, Froebel, James, and Dewey and you will find this unchanging core of agreement.

Rousseau's thoroughness results from the device he adopted for his exposition: a tutor who is explicitly described as a genius and a solitary child whose apparent freedom is rendered continuously productive by the genius in charge. Rousseau keeps repeating that the situation is not to be taken literally; it cannot be imitated, but its point and purpose can be understood. Everything that is shown as happening and everything Rousseau argues for suggests the true path; it is a map, not a photograph. There is a well-attested anecdote of the devotee who visited Rousseau and declared that having just become a father he was going to bring up his child exactly as prescribed in the *Emile*. Rousseau stared at him a moment and said: "That's too bad for you and your son. I never intended to supply a method, but only to remove the evils of contemporary education."

At the other end of the era that Rousseau and the Romantics inaugurated, the task of breaking up petrified schooling was once more necessary. Accordingly we find William James in the nineties applying his enormous psychological insight to the existing situation—a situation that had begun to be complicated by the presence of what he called "the softer pedagogy."

In *Talks to Teachers,* James tried with one hand to dispose of passive, undigested rote learning and with the other to show the error of coddling. He made it clear that children have minds as well as tender feelings, and that the methods and attitudes found useful with the very young should not be continued as the child matures. He showed that to respect the child, encourage his development, protect his individuality, and spur his self-teaching do not call for abolishing drudgery and competition or making no demands whatever.

Ten years later, Dewey's classic manual *How We Think* was equally uncompromising. The need for training, for precision, for hard work, for quiet concentration was steadily argued. One quotation among many should suffice to dispel the common misrepresentation of Dewey's thought: "Play should not be fooling . . . the only way of preventing this consequence is to make regard for results enter into even the freest play activity." All that is new or seems new in Dewey (much of it is already explicit in Rousseau) is the recommendation to make early instruction follow the pattern of scientific inquiry. Here James is wiser than Dewey, in seeing that it is as arbitrary to train the mind exclusively or largely to organize objects as it is to make it adept only at juggling words. In any case, James and Dewey agree on the essential need to know *something,* and to know it with the concreteness of perception and precision of imagination without which the verb to *know* is but a false pretense.

With the great thinkers on education cleared of the blame for nonsense, its actual sources can be dealt with. The minds that produce it would, if they turned to other subjects, produce equal nonsense of another kind. What makes its detection easy and quick is the very simplicity of the educational predicament to which I have drawn attention. Schools are always more or less in need of reform. Ossification is an ever-present danger. Rousseau and his peers offer remedies. But the remedies can be applied only within narrow limits. Rousseau's man of genius is not found on the membership lists of the teachers' associations, and to have a tolerable life, a child must grow up and learn with other children.

Thus the first producers of nonsense are the literalists. They confuse a philosophy with a recipe. Indeed, the great reservoir of educational nonsense is, first and last, confusion. And by confusion I do not mean mere mental chaos or bewilderment by great ideas but simple confounding—taking one thing for another.

For example, when Rousseau or Dewey suggests: let the child discover for himself, let him learn geometry and logic by struggling, let him teach himself—and I imagine every good teacher has in him the spirit of that injunction—the dedicated confounder makes of the hint a program. How many centuries would it take an ordinary child to rediscover by himself all the mathematics and sciences developed since Pythagoras? The pretense and folly of it is known as a "teaching experiment," of which the instances during the last 50 years have been numberless.

To a second confusion I have elsewhere referred as *preposterism.** Its prevalence is supported by the most delusive of devices, the so-called "study." A study shows that pupils do better work when their teachers believe in their ability. This is but the commonplace maxim that encouragement helps and that people tend to live up to the idea others have of them. But this truth is subject, of course, to the limitation of all statements of tendency: though some pupils profit from words of cheer, others work hard only under challenge or demand. But now the "study" prods teachers into hypocritical smiles, as if to mesmerize Suzie and John into doing better work.

The widespread idea that teaching can succeed in this way apart from a sincere relation, based on a genuine feeling, friendly or not, is the cause of an appalling amount of nonsense. Manipu-

*See below, pp. 83 ff. (Ed.)

lation in place of teaching is the cruelest and most harmful of false attitudes.

A second element at work is the belief in change and modernity. For 3,000 years children have been taught to read by sounding letters, one at a time, and taught to write by copying models; surely we can do better than that? But in fact there is no cruder mode of judging than that which asks: Is it new? The cult of the new has generated a mirage, in which have arisen all the schemes greeted with hope and forgotten in failure.

The layman meanwhile takes these fugitive novelties for the kind of quickening that the scholastic scene periodically needs. But it should not be hard to tell the difference between the two kinds. Innovation in the popular sense generally has something paradoxical, up-the-down-staircase, about it which immediately appeals to weak and jaded minds. Teaching high school seniors American history is, let us confess, hard work and it is not popular with the students. Who has a bit of innovation to apply to the sore spot? I have it! Let us teach the course backwards! The first lesson is the headlines in the daily paper—relevant enough to take your mind off your studies. Then you work your way back somehow to Christopher Columbus and the Vikings if graduation doesn't intervene.

All the fiddling with curriculum and scheduling belong to this same category of escape by faddishness: the unit, the project, the freshman seminar, the cross-fertilizing, the interdisciplinary program, and that will-o'-the-wisp, "independent work"—all sops to restlessness.

We see it today in the cry for Liberation. The open classroom in the lower schools has got rid of seats and desks, sees the ideal teaching situation as resembling the floor of the Stock Exchange on a busy day. In college, "liberation classes" are to be held outdoors in summer, for a humane diffusion of attention. In winter, students petition for the removal of fixed seats and do not consider chairs really free if equipped with a writing arm. They resent, besides, what they call the "humiliation of having their minds judged by a stranger at the end of the room." Examinations, grading are held to be degrading. Pass/fail is the sole acceptable report.

The confusion here is between the conditions of learning and those fancied as proper for a free citizen in an ideal world. For in the real world we have not yet got round to liberating the seats in buses and concert halls or removing the humiliating distinction between doctor and patient. On the contrary, alas, the modern world is more intent that ever on classification, identification numbers, and credentials—which is why, undoubtedly, the school feels the counterblow in these various pleas for the aboriginal free-for-all.

In truth, one generic confusion underlies all the particular confusions: the purpose of the school has been lost and buried under a multitude of secondary aims. The purely numerical need created by the great goal of mass education has shown that the supply of born teachers is entirely inadequate, not only to man the schools but to *uphold the idea of the school.*

That idea survived for a while in the universities. Now they too are in the hands of persons who want institutions of higher learning for almost any purpose but learning. Outside, there is no philosophic voice capable of making itself heard on the subject of teaching and learning. The voices we do hear give us undigested fragments of old doctrine thoroughly misunderstood, as I have tried to show. The only possible verdict about the school is: laziness, abdication, sham democracy and false equality, total absence of mind. If all this continues, the newest doctrine, launched by Father Illich, for the "deschooling of society," will be at once appropriate and unnecessary.*

*Ivan Illich, *Deschooling Society,* Harper and Row, New York, 1971.

their multiple meanings to one topic. Except when done by a ripe scholar, it is bound to be bits and pieces—no continuity and no context.

To appreciate the difficulty, take the adult profession of city planner. The knowledge it requires embraces items drawn from economics, sociology, demography, public health, architecture, landscaping, and engineering, as well as from law and government, local, state, and federal. The facts that are pulled out of these specialties can teach very little by themselves. Isolated, few will be remembered, and fitting them into a coherent pattern cannot be done by native wit alone.

Now most social studies courses did not even draw on such solid subjects; they made a hodgepodge of scattered data sprinkled with platitudes and pieties and then labeled so as to attract parents and youngsters: Family Living; Shopping and Community Resources; Values, Behavior, and Society. Whatever the stuffing, social studies reproduce this unworkable pattern. Even the old, much abused civics course, with its weekly supplement of "curnivents," showed better organization and continuity. Whatever the substance, to learn from composite studies presupposes long years of systematic work and much experience of life.

It may surprise you if I mention next as yet another instance of the pre-post fallacy the use of multiple-choice tests. My reason is this: it takes pretty thorough knowledge to detect error. Remember that in those tests the three wrong answers are made to look plausible. They are a piece of subtle deception practiced on minds that have just begun to acquire the outlines of a subject. The students have no sizable store of details with which to surround and defeat the falsehood. A scholar or a well-read reviewer will quickly spot a misstatement in what he reads in his own field, the reason it stands out being that it goes against a whole cluster of familiar facts. As Banesh Hoffmann showed in his investigation of testing, even Ph.D.'s with tenure at his own college made mistakes on the official sample test he persuaded them to take.* The student, the neophyte, is once again treated as a fully trained mind.

One last case: sex education. I am not concerned here with

* " 'Best Answers' or Better Minds?" *The American Scholar*, Spring 1959.

the question of giving or not giving such a course in public schools; that is another debate. I refer only to the way the subject is presented in some well-received programs. Teacher and textbook display to young people the whole range of adult sexuality, from its physiology and its personal, ethical, social, and medical consequences to the numerous variations it assumes in practice. All this is conveyed through film strips, color illustrations, and a surfeit of spoken words, for the manual tells the teacher to elicit opinions, preferences, expressions of feeling, and even confessions. It is hoped that by stimulating discussion as in group therapy, the teacher will put the members of the class at their ease on the great subject.

Now any adult who is familiar with the struggling emotions of late adolescence and its suspicion of inculcated facts, and who also reflects on the complexities of sexual behavior in civilized society, may well wonder at a program which not only invades privacy and promotes gossip, but which, in demanding self-analysis and philosophic ease, puts first what may, with luck, come last.

Having shown the ways in which modern schooling has been lured again and again to defy common sense, I must in fairness give some attention to what might be done instead. This means giving thought to the rudiments and the pedagogy that are being neglected—indeed, suppressed. And since mathematics has suffered the latest of the innovations I find harmful, it is the school subject on which I shall venture to offer some positive suggestions.

To begin with what I said earlier, the New Math includes one excellent idea: learners ought to be told the why of what they are asked to do. Endless operations done by rote are deadening. But of course the age of the pupil limits the kind and amount of reason that can be given. Good pedagogy says: to show connections is the best teaching, and connections imply something already present with which to link the new. So the first requisite in a math program is that each step should be mastered before going on to the next, just as each lesson ought to be next in some intelligible way.

The first step was decided on long ago: after learning the digits, the pupil is shown how to add, subtract, multiply, and divide. He or she must work *by hand* until these operations are done with the utmost facility—and the simpler ones mentally. The blanket objection to all rote learning and to frequent drilling is foolish. At the appropriate time, the multiplication table has to be learned, and the only way is by rote. No mastery in any subject is possible without much memorizing and practicing, from playing the piano to becoming a physician. But even with the multiplication table, noting some curious features can lend a bit of charm to the effort.

Nowadays any discussion of math in the schools raises an important question that must be met. The world of work complains that high school graduates can't do simple ciphering; corporations spend billions on remedial training. At the same time, the world of science often argues (though not always) that this "consumer math" is a waste of time. Now that hand calculators are cheap, let them do the operations while the young mind grapples with true mathematical difficulties. The boy or girl who will work in the supermarket can count on a cash register that adds and makes change; and the other pair, who will work in Bell Laboratories, will have had a proper grounding in the science of numbers.

This is the old quarrel between pure and applied mathematics. The famous Hilbert, at a world congress of mathematicians, opened the session by declaring that applied mathematics had nothing to do with pure mathematics, it never had had nor ever would have. When the New Math program was made public, it was avowedly an introduction to pure mathematics, and several distinguished applied mathematicians attacked it as utopian and predicted its failure. Meanwhile, there has been a continual outcry: the prestige and the economic health of the country require a steady supply of scientists; these must be accomplished mathematicians; therefore training appropriate to their future career must begin from the earliest grade. In turn, this is disputed by engineers and electronics wizards, who say that innovation comes not from mathematical insight but from a sense of "how things work." Mathematics is the medium of the generalizer, not of the inventor.

It is obviously impossible to foretell who will check out groceries and who will turn lasers to some new use. In any case, the public school has no choice but to teach the traditional arithmetic and its sequels, going from the four operations to fractions, decimals, percentage, the area of figures, factoring, simple equations, graphs and variables, and so on. For it must not forget the American people's ordinary occupations, including the mechanical trades, which are shamefully neglected in all the talk about public education.

The best reason for keeping hand calculators and computers out of the classroom is that their use leads to a know-nothing kind of ability, and a particularly crippling one. A calculator will go through steps rapidly and a computer will both solve complex equations and give quick results for changes in any of the terms. But the manipulative skill by which problems are fed to the machine does nothing to familiarize the learner with the successive forms that the step-by-step computation takes. Working out these steps by hand gives the mind that "feel of the material" which is essential to mastery in any art or trade. Schooling is meant to implant knowledge and skill, not the habits of the trained animal. Unless children are brought to see what they are doing when computing, the shopkeeper won't be able to tell when his cash register runs wild, and the artisan won't know which calculations could reduce his guesses to figures when he wants to save time, money, or materials. And there is also the white-collar commuter whose daily paper confronts him with graphs: he should know how to read them and draw the right conclusions.

As for the reasons by which the handling of numbers is to be justified so as to create interest and incentive, they fall into two groups—one is the finding of unknowns, a great set of tricks that is truly astonishing when well displayed. The other is the exposure of common fallacies—for example, the belief that a boundary line of a certain length will enclose the same area no matter what its shape. The teacher draws a square 10 inches to a side: the area is 100 square inches; then a rectangle 1 inch wide and 19 inches long. The latter has the same boundary length as the square: 40 inches, but its area is not 100, it is 19 square inches.

Advanced work consisting of geometry, algebra, and trigonometry is more effectively taught in parallel and overlapping fashion, as is done abroad, than one at a time in successive years. Connections are then more obvious, variety helps sustain interest, the methods of one science (e.g. algebra) when used in another are strengthened, and the underlying notions of logic, symmetry, and so on are seen as persuasive. Planning such a combined course to cover three years also reduces the amount of each component to its essentials, and the resulting saving of time may leave room in high school for a semester of calculus.

The creators of the new math were clear that their aim was to improve the teaching of science as well as that of arithmetic. But reform in that field did not follow and complaints continue as before. It is agreed fairly widely that "General Science" is as bad as Social Studies—a hodgepodge dished up, all too often, by incapable teachers. Yet public schools must in one sense remain "general;" they cannot specialize in the training of future scientists by giving them courses of professional quality. The school could neither require them nor expect more than a few to elect them.

The result of the present shoddy compromise is that most citizens are deplorably ignorant of the simplest scientific facts and ideas. They know nothing of the principles on which their familiar domestic machines work and they know less than nothing of the ways of the universe, for their minds often harbor ancient superstitions. They've heard of Newton and Einstein and there an end. The people of the despised Middle Ages knew more of their world-system than that, thanks to word-of-mouth tradition and church windows and sculpture that portrayed the great moments of the Christian religion.

The pivotal idea here is: world-system. Modern science forms a system, just as history forms a stream, and in both subjects the bits-and-pieces program is fatal to learning anything. There is no such thing as "general science" but there *is* a systematic way of introducing the scien*ces*. One excellent plan has been devised and tested by Wendell H. Taylor and his colleagues at the Lawrenceville School; it would be easy to adopt or adapt it, especially since they wrote a textbook for their own use.

Beginning in the seventh grade, that science curriculum takes the student in six years from the earth sciences through physics, chemistry, and biology, with electives at the end that permit an advanced course to be taken in any of these branches or their extension, e.g. astrophysics, genetics, meteorology. The necessary mathematics is given in parallel.

The logic of the plan is clear: one goes from the planetary system to matter as found on the earth (geology) to its behavior when handled and analyzed (mechanics, hydrostatics, electricity, etc.); then, to its inner composition (chemistry, inorganic and organic), and finally to its still higher organization in living things (biology). True, in one year only the rudiments of each science can be taught, but at the end these rudiments hang together, and the consecutive view of how matter behaves when looked at in different forms and places and with different techniques affords an intellectual experience of the cosmos as well as that rare thing nowadays, a *body* of knowledge.

For the future scientist, solid foundations are worth more than a scattering of miscellaneous information, no matter how far and wide the fragments may have reached. And for the citizen threading his way among an every-enlarging jungle of mechanical devices, it should be some satisfaction to know why they work— when they do. At present, he or she is probably unable to explain why one can grip an object harder with a pair of pliers than with the bare fingers, and how the use of electricity in a doorbell differs from its use in the television set.

As for what is meant by salt, acid, and base; how energy may be atomic and biology molecular, what is meant by composition of forces, magnetic field, or ultra-violet light, the answers would strike most people as taking them beyond what a normal human being should aspire to know. Yet a properly elementary treatment of the four sciences associated as at Lawrenceville would enable this vast public to see a host of familiar phenomena so to speak from the inside. Their workings would be remembered without effort, because their embodiments are on every side.

This pedagogical view, by the way, was the prevailing one early in this century, when physical science was touted as "organized common sense" and its proponents appealed to simple curiosity about the trees and the heavens, the steam engine and the telephone. Granted that this no longer suffices and the public thinks Newton's four laws have been "repealed," the former scheme has the merit of feasibility. Newton's laws are still on the books and ought to be in many minds.

What needs to be added to that earlier curriculum is an indication of the historical development of science—accounts of pivotal discoveries and formulations, of great figures and inspired guesses. It not only lends human interest to the work, but it shows the many ways the mind can take to reach data and frame laws. The road is not straight nor the advance steadily forward. Wrong assumptions, negative results have been important too. But all the while the goal has been single: to simplify and unify. All phenomena must be accounted for as parts of a system in which a few forces act uniformly. All particular differences will then be explained by position, time, and quantity.

The goal of schooling bears a direct relation to this great goal of the scientist. Remember that schooling should begin at the beginning and not set out with hopeful endings; that it should make use of reasons and ideas, but not neglect memory and practice; that it should concentrate on rudiments so as to give a body of knowledge to some and the foundations of higher studies to others—well, what is the goal of such schooling? It is to turn out men and women who are not wide-eyed strangers in a world of wonders, but persons whose understanding of what they see makes them feel more at home in our inescapably double environment, natural and man-made.

8

The Art of Making Teachers

INTRODUCTORY

Now that the collapse of the American public school is admitted on all hands, after thirty years of blindness on one side and defensive lying on the other, attention has turned to the question, What about the teachers—are they to blame or are they victims too? And the related question follows, Where should we turn for good teachers? For shortage is added to the other woes, and some states have begun to certify graduates of liberal-arts colleges. The emergency has also prompted a movement called Teach for America, which appeals to a praiseworthy idealism in the young. It looks like an opportunity to break the stranglehold of the educationists on teacher training and the teacher mind.

Strange as it may seem, it is a fact of nature that there are more born poets than born teachers. But the world's work cannot depend on genius; it must make do with talent, that is to say, fair material properly trained. Up to now teacher training has been done by people unfitted for the job, by temperament and by purpose. By temperament they have no interest in Learning or capacity for it; by purpose they are bent not on instruction but on social work. They care little about history or science or good English, but they grow keen about any scheme of betterment; one recent proposal is: teach the importance of washing the hands.

The result of half a century or more of this world-reforming attitude may be seen in the language in which educationists think and talk. A fair sampling appears in the discussion of art teaching that follows this note. It characteristics are: abstraction instead of direct naming; exaggeration of goals and results; seeing the stu-

96

dent not as an individual but as an example of some psychological generality; taking any indirect means in place of the straight one; and finally: mistaking words for facts, and intentions for hard work.

Such is the educationist mind everywhere. A few years ago New York City, finding its school system in bad shape, set up a task force to look into the trouble and devise remedies. After a time, a large gathering of interested and qualified persons was invited to hear of any progress made. An impressive and fluent woman official took about an hour to describe the committee's procedure, summarize its report, and explain how the recommendations worked to reform the whole system. Then she asked for questions. One bold spirit ventured "Could you tell us what success you have had so far?" The answer: "We have had complete success. All the heads of department to whom we sent the report have replied that it met with their full approval."

Nothing happened, of course. The system is in worse shape than ever, though an able superintendent is trying to force the conversion of words into acts. The educationist spirit is that of bureaucracy—marks on paper take precedence over reality—and bureaucracy is inconvertible. Indeed, some observers have lately said that no system, anywhere in the country, can be changed. Physicists can transmute the chemical elements but not the schools.

What is the origin of this subculture which defies American practicality by shielding its malpractice behind a repellent vocabulary? It has long been known that nearly all college students who want to become teachers and who as seniors elect the education courses required for certification, fall back discomfited by what they are asked to learn. Though young and moved by a generous impulse, they can see that the "methods" taught are mere word-spinning and that while the relation of method to subjects is nonexistent, subjects themselves are the last concern of educationism.

In short, teacher training is based on a strong anti-intellectual bias, enhanced by a total lack of imagination. The trainers live in a thick cloud of nomenclature, formulas, "objectives," evaluations, and "strategies." By instinct, it seems, doing is held at arm's length; any call for change starts with a pompous windup: "When we talk about goals, we imply a context for action that transcends a dictionary definition. Institutional planning embraces mission, goals, and objectives, while business strategic planning defines roles, goals, and tactics. Goals . . . theoretically can be commonly defined and shared so that everyone is heading in the right direction."

To most teachers this mode of thought is or becomes second nature; the school-teaching profession believes in fantasy. It would be wrong to say that the young recruits are brainwashed— they are brain*soiled*. No doubt strong minds escape the blight, but they must go on to do their good teaching despite the creed and its oppressive atmosphere.

What then are the native qualities to look for in the person who, though not one of those born to the task, would make a good teacher? And what sort of training should such a person get? As to the first requirement: brains enough to feel bewildered and revolted by the educationist language—and courage enough to admit it. Next, a strong interest in some branch of learning, meaning any one of the genuine school subjects. Which those are can be found every day in the newspaper articles that bewail the failure of the schools. Nobody writes about the poor showing in "Shopping and Community Resources."

In addition, a teacher should have some interests beyond his or her specialty. In bearing, in manner of thinking and talking, a teacher should quite naturally appear to be a person with a mental life, a person who reads books and whose converse with colleagues is not purely *business* shop; that is, not invariably methods and troubles, but substance as well. There is no hope of attracting students to any art or science and keeping up their interest without this spontaneous mental radiation. When it is reported that the teaching of biology imparts nothing but a rooted dislike of science, it is easy to see what disconnection exists between the mind of the teacher and the nature of the subject.

A key phrase in the foregoing is *naturally have a mental life*. It implies that the teacher *likes* books and ideas. With these likes, the teacher will not become a fussy pedant or a tense martinet and will avoid another failing now often seen: false modesty and self-consciousness. Addressing parents, a teacher from a very good school confides: "Teaching is part performance, part prat-fall—at least, my teaching is so. I never know what's coming when I go into a class." Then resign and take a less scary job. But the words are insincere—conventional hokum to show that the speaker is not highbrow or know-it-all, that a teacher is only a person older than his students, not wiser or better informed—"we all learn together." (The cliché that a teacher learns from his students is true, but the thing learned is not at all the same and it is not a continuous "course.")

Now suppose a young woman, a young man, with a good mind and normal common sense, who is eager to become a teacher. Training to fulfill this ambition calls for nothing complicated or abstruse. The all-important thing is mastery of a subject matter. Ideally, it should be the freely chosen major in college; or, if lacking a college degree, the trainee should have done well in that subject in high school. A longer course will then bring him up to par.

This main subject needs to be supplemented by courses in other fields, to give awareness of their contents and outlook and their relation to the main subject. Providing this "environment" is the ancient goal of a liberal education, which may be likened to a map of the mental life with one region of it extremely familiar, because it is "home." For the teacher, a history of educational theories would complete the program. It should be made clear, too, that science and mathematics are liberal arts, not some mystery of recent growth and suddenly in demand "for the 21st century."

Speaking of science, should the teacher learn psychology, child psychology in particular? No. The science, which is by no means settled, is like other sciences; it yields only generalities; and teaching is par excellence the adaptation of one particular mind to another. There is no such thing as *the* child—at any age. Teaching is not the application of a system, it is an exercise in perpetual discretion. One pupil, too timid, needs to be cheered along; another calmed down for the sake of concentration. Correcting faults and errors must take different forms (and words) in individual cases and must usually be accompanied by praise for the good achieved. Variety of tasks is indicated for some and steady plugging for others. The class is not to be spoken to in the same way as the single child, and fostering emulation must not generate anxious competitiveness.

Now, no method on earth will teach ahead of time when, how, and to whom these purposely contrary acts are right or wrong. Intuition—for want of a better term—is the true guide. A good teacher can spot a gifted child without learning the twenty-two characteristics listed in *The Encyclopedia of Education.* * The few pointers of a general sort that would help a prentice teacher can be found in William James's *Talks to Teachers,* a small book still in print after nearly a century.

The way to learn the art of teaching is by imitation. To teach well one should have had at least one good teacher and been struck, consciously or not, by the means employed and the behavior displayed. It follows that practice teaching is an indispensable part of the training. But here lies the appalling predicament of the present hour: how can imitation and practice teaching produce anything but the kind of teachers we have had, misdirected and miseducated, as Koerner warned so long ago? Unless bypassed, the profession will perpetuate, in all good faith and with heart-melting slogans, the damnable errors that have killed instruction and made the classroom a center for expensive waste.

The discussion that follows shows in detail how the profession thinks about one standard subject and thus the reality of the impasse.

* Volume 6, p.156.

Occupational Disease:
Verbal Inflation

National Art Education Association, Houston, March 18,
1978; *Art Education*, October 1978; *Journal of Aesthetic
Education,* October 1978; *Art in Basic Education,*
Washington: Council for Basic Education, March 1979

G lad as I am to be with you, and flattered by your invitation, what I feel even more keenly is the rashness of my accept- ance. The cause of this feeling is the present chaotic state of opinion about art and art education in this country. Every- where, thoughtful, earnest people concerned with the issues seem irreconcilable partisans, even though the issues are anything but clearly drawn. Like most other divisions of instruction, the teach- ing of art in the public schools shows nothing approaching same- ness in method or substance. It varies from excellent to make- believe, from superb to absurd. The demand for it varies likewise from zero to intense. What is worse, in a time of scarce money, the arts can be readily shown as frills easy to cut off; and again, the movement called Back to Basics is seen by some as a threat to courses in the arts, while others, like the Council for Basic Edu- cation, of which I am a director, list art among the basics. Lastly, there is not—there has never been—agreement upon the reasons for giving the arts room in the curriculum. Is it for self- expression, appreciation, a future career? Or is it for the arts' intellectual contents, historical importance, or manifest role in a high civilization?

Amid this Babel, I cannot hope to say anything that will please you all; I may in fact *dis*please you all, for I am going to say more than one thing, and each remark may alienate in turn some part of this audience, until I find myself in need of a body- guard. However it turns out, you may be sure of two facts. One is that I think the arts should be taught in the schools. The second is that my purpose is not to teach you your own business, but possi- bly—just possibly—lift a burden from your minds, a load of anxiety and of imaginary duties, created precisely by the causes of the present confusion.

Let us at once face the difficult position of the arts in any general school, that is, a school not exclusively devoted to one art—music school, drama school, or art school. That difficult position is inherent and due to three things—the use of time, the uneven distribution of talent, and the absence of standards other than professional. Take these together concretely: in a specialized school, most students are gifted, they are keen to learn, want to spend long stretches of time practicing, and the teacher is free to judge progress in the light of future professional competence. In a general school, right up through college, none of these conditions survives integration with the rest of the curriculum. The gifted are held to a few scattered hours and vague requirements, and the ungifted see no reason for the useless, "elitist" stuff they are asked to study.

Why then did the arts ever come into the general schools? One reason—the best reason—is that in every generation boys and girls are born with artistic talent, and some with a drive toward developing it. Except at school—a public school—most of these children would never get a chance to discover the gift or fulfill their desire. Moreover, if gifted, they should be taught while their minds, muscles, and senses are still plastic. Nothing makes up for the lack of early training of the eye, ear, throat, and fingers.

But in recent times other reasons have been added. The belief has grown that everybody regardless of talent should become acquainted with art. With the decline of traditional religion the cult of art has taken its place in the heart and mind of Western man. Art is now held to be mankind's highest form of spiritual expression. The devotees of high art say they find through it a unique harmonizing of the emotions; the devotees of popular art visibly find in it a means of social communion.

Several further arguments reinforce this unprecedented valuation of art. Some are discussed in the widely read report called *Coming to Our Senses*, which I am sure you all know. There is, first, the contention that both schooling and daily life overdo the

use of words and practical knowledge, and that we should culti-
vate, at least as much, other modes of thought and expression.
Then there is the cliché that the world has "gone visual." With
television to picture things and computers to figure things out for
us, words are said to have become almost unnecessary. Yet from
an opposite corner it is urged that we need art to resist the influence of just these technological wonders. As in Lewis Mumford's
recantation about the machine as a model for architecture, art has
come to be represented as a necessary humanizer of life, a sooth-
ing balm for our bruised spirits. Writers on education have taken
up the cry for exploring a realm where things are not measurable,
literal, or useful, but purely "lyrical"—intuitive, figurative,
imaginative, and hence good for our souls.

This notion of a balanced diet is very sound, but the reasoning is less so. Surely art and science, language and technology are
all equally products of humanity, none "more human" than another. And when you reflect that our modern cultivation of music
and painting is carried on with hi-fi and cassettes, slide projectors
and color reproductions—all of them fruits of technology—you
see that there is no getting away from the machine. But the use of
it is in our control. We are not compelled to look at television or
to go visual and musical because television uses pictures and music—both with many words; nobody would look at TV ten minutes if it were all in dumb show.

Besides, among those who want the arts to heal the wounds
dealt by technology are some who worship science and see in the
teaching of art a spur to problem-solving. They maintain that
great artists and great scientists work the same way: by intuition
under the control of technique, by observing things closely and
making patterns among them; and so we hear rhapsodies about
the beauty of mathematics and physics rivalling that of frescoes
and symphonies. Finally, a few voices are heard to say that literature, which uses the now disfavored word, is also an art, where
images, intuition, patterns, and other "lyrical," non-quantitative
elements are to be found; and these people wonder whether literature, including poetry, is still taught as an art in the modern
school.

As you see, the chaos and confusion starts in the world outside the classroom—and who should blame it? It is a permanent trait of the world to be a smoky battleground of good and bad arguments. What is deplorable is that the school—I mean those in charge of that great institution, men and women presumably trained to work with ideas and coordinate means and ends— should be in similar or worse confusion; that they should waste their time in endless debate over the same points and thereby misdirect their efforts; the net result being a chorus of mutual recrimination. One says, for example, that a particular branch of art education is "worthless pap" and that he would "rather see it go out of the curriculum than continue as it is." To which another replies that "in amount and quality that teaching is the best in the Western world." And a third opines that "nobody ever likes the way anyone else teaches the subject." Worst of all, the general public utters more and more freely its discontent with all teaching, convicts it of failure, and no longer trusts those in charge, supposedly expert.

This outcome of the battle of ideas is very grave. It threatens the public school itself, the arts and the teachers of art, together with the welfare of the young entrusted to their hands.

How did the American people, the practical people who created the public school and made it work, get to such a pass? The answer is: Inflation—not monetary inflation, but intellectual, emotional, social, egotistical inflation. For the last fifty years, American Education has pursued a policy of overstatement about its role and substance; it has lived by continual exaggeration of what it is for and what it can do. The medium naturally is words, words misunderstood and misapplied—it is verbal inflation.

As in the worst sort of advertising, whatever Education offers is said, ahead of time, to be the latest and best, most perfect, supreme; the results of its use are glorious, incomparable, magnificent. In the literature of Education, what is taught and the benefits that follow are always universal in scope; the authors acknowledge no limits; they will not tell the truth nor face simple facts. They suspend common sense and fly to metaphors and abstractions to cover the genuine things that can be done, that could be done, if they were not addicted to educational guff. If you doubt my word, read your top-heavy curriculum plans, your twelve objectives and your twenty-three guidelines, and bring to mind the dozens and scores of fraudulent slogans with which our profession has gargled during the last two generations, swinging this way and that between equally unreal panaceas, now all gone with the wind of which they were made.

The error began with the replacement of the word *pedagogy* with the word *education*. Pedagogy is not a beautiful word, but it sticks to the point of teaching. It denotes the art of leading a child to knowledge, whereas education properly refers to a completed development, or the whole tendency of the mind toward it. A person is taught by a teacher but educates him- or herself, partly by will, partly by assimilating experience. The educator's egotistical urge to blur this distinction is at the root of our present predicament. Thinking that we can "*give* an education," we make wild claims and promises and forget to teach what is teachable. Babbling incessantly, we grope toward the remote, ill-defined, unattainable goals that fill our blatant advertising.

On the particular subject of our concern, look critically at what is said in current discussions of art for the schools. Here is a short list of the aims: to develop esthetic potential—what is that but vague and pretentious talk? to transmit the cultural heritage—how can this possibly be done in one course? to supply an outlet for self-expression—this is impossible before technique is mastered; to give a chance of success to non-verbal minds—good, but success in which art and to what degree? to enlarge the understanding of Man—does this really come out of modeling clay or playing in the band? to master a system of symbols—this may do for reading music but not for painting or any form of design; to fill out the outline of history, which is incomplete without art—that implies art history, not art in practice; to acquaint the child with foreign cultures—that would mean comparing styles after much familiarity with one's own; to show that not everything is quantifiable—this can be done while teaching English composition, American history, or any foreign language; to enhance achievement in other subjects—why use art for this purpose instead of pep pills or free hamburgers? to counterbalance utilitarian subjects—who says that playing drums or drawing cans of tomato soup can't be utilitarian?

These stated goals are bad enough, but trailing after them is a batch of slogans supposed to organize the lust for art: teach a sensory language; communicate creatively; visual (musical) literacy; social studies enrichment; engender general creativeness; build ethnic identity; enhance problem-solving; humanise schooling; give creative vision; achieve affective education. This last, according to one enthusiast, is interpreted to mean that "it is more important to feel rightly than to think rightly." What a false dilemma! Must one be either a fool or a knave? And if one feels rightly, does it not imply some thought which is also right? Why so many irresponsible words?

It is all Inflation. If inflates the plausible or possible into the miraculous. And remember that this collection of vague, vacuous, lofty, unexamined phrases is not taken from as many plans expressing different hopes. One document contains eighteen such purposes, all to be gone after and realized by any one school program. Several other programs list six or eight of these wonder cures. None connect any slogan or objective with any particular activity recognizable as teaching art. What this fatal gap means is that art—the most concrete, tangible, sensuous business in the world—art becomes an abstraction, a great white cloud showering on us by magic six or ten or eighteen golden benefits.

Now compare with the hazy vistas of the inflationists something known to have happened. Under one art program sponsored from outside, a master dancer and drummer from Ghana came to a sixth-grade class "to focus on the arts of Africa for two weeks" (decide for yourselves what "focus" means). During that time (I quote) the class "created African art of their own." Thanks to another scheme, the federal program called Artists-in-Schools, a professional weaver was sent to a school where six students were excused from music class for eight weeks to study her craft. According to one report, the course "concentrated on technique rather than creativity, appreciation, or the history of the art."

Here at last we have two bits of reality, in contrast with all the inflated descriptions. But don't mistake the point of the contrast. I am not saying the weaver and the drummer did the right thing—or the wrong thing, either. I am saying that these are the modest little events blanketed under the usual verbiage of "catalyst for general creativity" and "exciting introduction of a new dimension in the school."

Is it not now clear that even when something actual, positive is done about art in a class, the inflationary temper immediately works distortion and confusion upon the facts? Take first the prostituted word, "creative." Think of the Creation, by God or Chance—making something where nothing was before; something new, unexampled, fresh and fit to arouse wonder. To me, the wonder of artistic creation is so great that creative is a sacred word, forbidden except to describe extraordinary achievements. I find it offensive to African art that in two weeks a sixth-grade class *created* "African art *of their own.*"

Similarly, in the judgment passed on the weaver, one can see how completely school people have lost the sense of reality. How could that craftswoman have taught in eight weeks the history of the art? How can any such course do anything but show some small part of one kind of weaving? And until various kinds are shown and compared, how can "appreciation" occur? The disappointed tone of the comment is a measure of educational illusionism—those eight weeks did not transmit the cultural heritage, enrich the social studies, fill out the picture of history, teach a new sensory language, humanise schooling, or acquaint the students with other cultures. All it did was excite them like an unexpected party—and keep them away from the art of music.

In truth, the language of all these proposals, discussions, and reports verges on the insane. What is *general* creativity? Do we say "general championship"? Or is the champion the one who has in fact won the title in a particular sport? Again, if art is to "humanise schooling" are we admitting that the rest of the curriculum is inhuman? Art as an antidote to schooling means we first poison the young and then make them cough up the dose with an elective.

Do not comfort yourselves with the thought that nothing more is involved here than professional jargon which a purist is taking exception to. I am dealing not with detachable words but with the substance of attitudes and actions. Through the ideas that I bring to your consciousness and try to make you see as deplorable you cripple your teaching, for the ideas misdirect it. And you deceive your students by false promises raising false hopes. You pretend to be in a state of uninterrupted orgasmic euphoria while actually in a condition of perpetual impotence.

Look at some of those unthinking words again: the verbal is said to be overstressed, but we are asked to teach visual *literacy* and a sensory *language*. Language and literacy refer to words and nothing else. The metaphor that applies them to artistic matters is false and misleading; it destroys the case for art, whose rightful claim to special merit is that it is a mode of thought without words, *in*-articulate, *sui generis*. This mania for misnaming, this love of fog is infectious and I regret to add that one of the best writers on our subject was led by it to suggest that the goal of a good education in art should be: "how to create, confront and criticize works of art"; that is to say, give evidence of a triple power that only a few geniuses in each generation can be said to possess.

These fantasies and the meager facts behind them drive one to an obvious conclusion. If we cannot organize in our heads a few solid ideas about art in the world and art in the classroom, then the sooner we give up planning and theorizing the better. No use palavering about "affective education" when we are so far from any sort of effective education—and not only in art: 23 million functional illiterates are among us mutely reproaching us for our sins of inflation.

Such is also the view of sensible citizens, of parents on the school boards and the tax rolls. I quote one of them who a few months ago wrote to the Council for Basic Education, precisely about teaching art. He said: "I don't believe any thoughtful person is 'out to get art' because it is art. The thing that bothers most of us lay people is that we do not share the confidence of educators that, on the one hand, the three R's seem so difficult to teach, so subtle to introduce, so impossible to measure true progress in; and yet on the other hand the teaching of such subjective disciplines as art, current events, and movie-making is so straightforward and easy. . . . If the core curriculum were demonstrably well taught, the lay public would trust educators to attempt teaching art as well."

That is clear and candid speech—no ulterior motive, no

partisanship for one or another doctrine. The man tells those of us who believe in teaching art what we are up against. And he confirms the connection I have made between our special subject and the general corruption of pedagogy by the abstract, the grandiose, and the impossible. Through the inflation of terms and of our own egos we ourselves have raised up the obstacles we perpetually groan about. We have forgotten that like governing, teaching is the art of the possible.

What then is the remedy? It is obvious, in plain sight, staring us in the face. We must sober up; give up getting drunk on hope and verbiage; stop writing committee reports, guidelines, objectives. Mimeographed paper is the hard drug of the educational world. All those words ending in -tion and -ive are narcotics that break down the mind permanently. There do not have to be eighteen reasons to justify art in the school. One is enough. Let it be put this way: "Art is an important part of our culture. It corresponds to a deep instinct in man; hence it is enjoyable. We therefore teach its rudiments."

Do a good job of teaching them and what happens after that is none of your business. No teacher, no "educator" has a right to expect—much less to demand—those miraculous results, those improvements and transformations of the human soul. We are not gods, or even demigods, that we should dare push and pull, manipulate and mold others into the ideal image we have formed of the artist, or the connoisseur, or the cultivated man, whose senses are polished like a keyboard for art to play a tune on. To be or not to be such a person is each living being's private concern.

Give up utopianism, get sober and stay sober, and think of all the released time at your disposal, clear of committee meetings and the reading of reports. Think of all the restored energy, free from wild or platitudinous guidelines. The serious energy crisis of our day is that with so much human effort expended, the nation gets so little real work done—in business, in government, in the schools. We are busy bodies and low achievers.

This earnest suggestion of mine—to cut down by an act of will the verbal and mental inflation which denatures every purpose in education—that suggestion is what I hoped might lift a

burden from you; might relieve anxiety and lessen toil by removing a dead load of pseudo-thought and pseudo-work. You need
not fear that if you act on it you will cause unemployment—except perhaps among the pure verbalizers, who by dint of believing
their own advertisements have become incapable of the real work
which is teaching and supervising.

But good or bad, my suggestion does not tell you what to
do, and without some indicated path you can hardly muster new
courage and strength for the real work I keep referring to. True,
yet I am confident that many of you already have implicit answers
to the question, What to do? and I am sure that when you are
liberated from present theoretical shackles, the results will be better than what has been. Even so, I should like to recommend to
both the self-assured and the hesitant that they start with an act
which our crowded lives rarely permit—to think. To think, not
with the aid of books or articles or studies, but nakedly, with the
bare mind; and again, to think not lofty thoughts in big words, as
if for publication, but think plainly and privately; don't get up on
a ladder, but think like Richard II when he said: "For God's sake,
let us sit upon the ground and tell sad stories of the death of
kings." Sit on the ground and tell yourself what you know—what
you know about art, about teaching, about people young and old.

Trust your common sense, keeping away from the old
grooves of educational piety, and you will make some interesting
discoveries, reach conclusions you can rely on, because they
come out of your whole experience and not your slogans and
shoptalk. Consider, for example, the idea of Art. What do *you*
think it covers? Well, music and painting and sculpture, of course;
and the dance and—oh, literature, also. (So easy to forget literature when it's called English or composition or language arts.) But
does Art include acting, scene-painting, directing, film-mak-
ing, journalism, broadcasting, photography, weaving, pottery,
jewelry-making, batik, macramé?—the list can be long if Art includes all the crafts.

While pondering the list, you can amuse yourself by matching any item—say photography—against the current "objectives"
of humanizing technology, building up a sensory language, or ex-
tending the taste for lyrical emotion. But the serious question to

ask yourself is, Which of all the nameable arts and crafts are in fact teachable in school? None completely, that is sure. The school cannot turn out a painter, a weaver, or a film-maker, no matter how much talent and drive is present at the start. It is sure also that in the greater number there will be little or no such talent. These two facts lead one to wonder whether any fundamentals can be found that underlie several forms of art. Is there something which is to the arts what arithmetic is to the higher mathematics, what reading and writing are to literature and all other written discourse? Clearly, the rudiments of music serve in just that way the dancer, singer, and instrumentalist, as well as the composer, critic, and amateur of music. Likewise drawing serves all the arts and crafts that consist of making visual patterns. The photographer and film-maker work with design as much as the sculptor, architect, scene-painter, weaver, jeweler, or dress-maker. What is more, the rudiments are equally useful in the sophisticated and in the popular form of every art.

In these two sets of rudiments, then, we seem to have got hold of the practical roots of all the arts except literature. The special use that each art makes of the fundamentals varies indefinitely and the school cannot begin to teach all the applications. To teach some and not others would mean an arbitrary choice, needlessly enforced on students who might prefer some other arts or crafts. Why not open the way to the full range of later individual interest by concentrating on the root disciplines? In other words, why not the basics in art too? If you think a moment about that ugly word, you will see that what it means in effect is: The teachables—what can actually be taught in a general school, the common ground of mental and physical activity that is the foundation of all self-development, self-expression, and self-satisfaction.

It is not my place to tell you in detail what the rudiments of music and design are, much less how to go about teaching them at the several stages of human growth. All I permit myself to say is that if one begins the right teaching early enough, all normal children can acquire the habits on which these two of the three great divisions of art build their structures. For habits is all that the basic powers consist of: bodily habits—of the eye, the ear, and the hand. I do not believe that any ear, caught young, is incurably tone-deaf, and I do believe that any one who can learn to write can learn to draw—and might write a better-looking hand in consequence.

All this, you may say, is academic stuff. How do we teach the children to be original, innovative? You don't; you can't. Originality is not teachable. Academic is what teaching ought to be in an academy. The great innovators start from there, and they innovate to good purpose when they have reached the limits of academic skill or when, through a special gift, they modify unconsciously the physical habits that are basic to design or the art of sounds. The results embody an acquired skill and not simply the first vagaries of the dabbler.

You may ask, But where in all this is the fun? Sight-reading, taking dictation of intervals and rhythms, learning to sing or play in tune; and again, learning to draw in perspective, to copy in various mediums, and use colors in the light of theory is nothing but hard work, much of it drill, and some of it learning by rote. So it is; so it should be. Only by demanding hard work will the arts escape the charge of being an expensive and expendable frill. Only so will they achieve tangible results. Nor does this principle apply only to art. The sole justification of teaching, of the school itself, is that the student comes out of it able to do something he could not do before. I say *do* and not *know,* because knowledge that doesn't lead to doing something new or doing something better is not knowledge at all.

Before you give me up as a slave-driver, think once more. The two sets of rudiments I have defined do not exist as bare bones, except temporarily for pedagogy. In reality, they are embedded in pieces of genuine art, even when the pieces are simple and easy to grasp. Children will respond to singing them, copying them, coloring them, analyzing them, once the means have been put into their hands and their heads. All new powers bring enjoyment to the possessor, and the extra-curricular uses of power over sound and rhythm, over color and line are so many and so obvious that nobody need worry that this mode of art teaching will fail to bring pleasure. What should be worried about is the course that leads nowhere because it aims only to please, by fooling around with art, by make-believe about self-expression and creativity, by improvising African art in two weeks. Such schemes of shreds and patches and playing at serious subjects is what has brought down the high repute of the American public school.

Our only hope is to fight our way back, win back our good name, by thinking straight and working hard and never forgetting that all the school subjects are members one of another, born and created equal within the single mind of man. There is good reason for music and the graphic arts to expect from their students competent arithmetic and some knowledge of other peoples, times, and places. And both these branches of art must also make demands on their third sister, literature, the English language now in dire straits from abuse and neglect. Sensitivity to words is part of pedagogy at large, as it has been my ungrateful task to demonstrate today by contrasting slogans with facts. But words—correct words—are also indispensable to the teaching of art. Critical judgment, appreciation, stylistic analysis, disputation about tastes, historical comparisons, and efficient instruction itself depend on the appropriate use of words. Indeed, except for the handful of students who become professional artists after a grounding in the public school, the benefits of teaching art to the young will consist mainly in the pleasure that comes of being able to see and hear works of art more sharply and subtly, more consciously, to register that pleasure in words, and compare notes with other people similarly inclined. The cultivation of the arts is a social as well as an individual enterprise, which is a second reason why its beginnings, however difficult to teach, properly belong among the teaching duties of the school.

9

The Word: Written, Printed, Spoken

The screening committee had to interview 150 young people—three top students from each state—and award to ten of them full college scholarships, each worth $60,000. One member of the committee asked every candidate this question: "Did you, during the past year, read a book that was not assigned? If so, please tell us a little about that book." Only one student out of the 150 was able to comply.

From evidence of this sort many have concluded that Americans do not read. The prophets of a generation ago must have been right when they said that hereafter all communication would be by broadcast picture and voice. Let us bury Gutenberg and his movable type.

That cheerful vision is contrary to fact. People read more than ever, as will appear a little further on. They have to read, because both the tasks and the pleasures of life require more and more information, and that information is in manuals, catalogues, reports, fact sheets, newsletters, and magazines. Though the editor of the *Harvard Business Review* defined her journal as "written by people who can't write for people who won't read," specialist magazines multiply incessantly, while print remains a medium for local news, domestic advice, and advertising.

Is the truth then that Americans do not read *books*? No, not that either. They read tons of books—again, of the informative kind—travel books, for example, and the many others that rehash current events or give "the story behind." What they rarely read is real books. As the 149 students showed, schooling does not give them the habit.

How is "real book" defined? Quite simply: it is a book one wants to reread. It can stand rereading because it is very full—of ideas and feelings, of scenes and persons real or imagined, of strange accidents and situations and judgments of behavior: it is a world in itself, like and unlike the world already in our heads. For this reason, this fullness, it may well be "hard to get into." But it somehow compels one to keep turning the page, and at the end the wish to reread is clear and strong: one senses that the work contains more than met the eye the first time round.

Now the point of reading books habitually is that it affords lasting pleasure, so the school should at least give every child a chance of contracting the habit. But it is not the adult citizen's *duty* to read good books, even if Mark Twain did point out that "the man who does not read good books has no advantage over the man who cannot read them."

Meanwhile, everybody agrees that it is desirable, indeed profitable in a business sense, to write acceptably; and this the school cannot teach without making the child read real books. For the main difficulty in teaching writing is to make the student conscious of words. In reading everyday prose, just as in listening to others speaking, the mind is wholly employed in absorbing the sense. The means by which sense is conveyed escape notice entirely. Writing reverses the situation: the mind must find words-as-such and fit them to the desired sense. How awkward this struggle is can be heard in common talk; it is full of "hm's" and "er's" and backtracking and muddled phrases that require a "What do you mean?" In every corner of life, trouble is accounted for by this ever-present "failure of communication." The root cause: clear utterance has never been made conscious and easy by practice— and that same lack makes for bad listening.

In books by great writers it is the very difficulty they present, the remoteness from jargon and clichés, that do the work of waking up the student to the role of words. Once made alive to the work and ways of words singly and in groups, the student begins to find writing possible. This awareness presupposes that the exact use of terms and the adroit management of syntax found in well-written books has been discussed in detail by the teacher.

These verbal elements become interesting by simple comparison. It is a fact of experience that once alerted to such things, anybody will grow curious about language: Why does this mean thus-and-so here and something else there? What if the sentence read this way? Why would it sound funny if it were turned around, with the last clause first? How is it we can often tell formal from colloquial but not always? And so on. The language columns in newspapers and in *The Readers' Digest* show that the interest is not a rarity.

The first gain for writing in well-taught reading is an enlarged vocabulary. The second is the perception that arrangement controls meaning. The third comes from familiarity with correct idiom and connotation. Both speech and writing are ultimately copy-cat performances—wordings get in through the ear or the eye and come out at the tongue or the end of a pencil. So it is sensible to make the source of *un*conscious expression the best available.

The conscious effort aims at self-criticism. Since nobody can write an acceptable first draft, good writing is always rewriting. And to rewrite or revise, one must have, on top of word consciousness, a bag of tricks for making repairs. Some may wonder: "If the books read for 'composition' are these good books that are read for 'literature,' isn't the writing going to be stilted, old-fashioned, ridiculous? Today, no good writer writes like Lincoln or Thoreau or even Mark Twain. Better take more recent models." This usually means *Catcher in the Rye*, with which the boys and girls so readily "identify."

That is just the trouble. It takes no imagination to feel at home in contemporary books, hence the language they use remains transparent—not there *as such*. As for students writing sentences like the classic models, never fear! They do not *think* like Lincoln or Thoreau; they do not become poets after reading Shakespeare. What they absorb and make use of are the good strong words and idioms, the clear structures, and the ways to link ideas. These are the eternal elements of good writing.

The real danger, on the contrary, is that teachers will make war on simplicity and plainness and require essays that sound like what *they* read in that language of education which is all their own. Some years ago, a member of the English department at the University of Chicago made a survey of writing done at the local high schools. He found that the good marks were given to students who wrote like the educationist models handed out to them, while the low marks went to those who wrote the true vernacular, often with lapses of grammar and tone, but surely with a better instinct for what prose should be.

Correcting the weekly essays is of course a taxing duty. It is not enough to mark errors; their nature and cause must be indicated, either in the marginal note or in class, orally. Ways to avoid faults, too, have to be shown, since mistakes come in typical forms. In short, there are principles to be stated that will serve as preventive medicine. All this teaching demands writing ability, and one is not surprised to read that one recent and successful effort begins by making teachers also write. If from now on they are to write, as well as read student work, the class must be of manageable size. At present, the student-teacher ratio averages 17.6, the highest being 22.9. Neither precludes the desirable degree of individual attention.

There remains the difficulty of getting the pupils to write at all. Telling them how useful proficiency will be is wasted breath; writing's a nuisance now, the future will take care of itself. What of the urge to self-expression? It moves only a few; the rest take it out in shouting during playtime. No doubt about it, writing is an artificial endeavor. No boy wants to describe his visit to Aunt Sally, no girl feels eager to pretend "I am the Mississippi. I am at first a small stream flowing amid . . ." There are no congenial subjects, whether assigned or left to choice, that will regularly yield the wanted page-and-a-half.

The best way out is to turn the student mind from substance to technique. One great void in writing instruction everywhere is that it does not show how one begins. The assumption is that given a topic, the child will quickly summon up ideas, after which the words flow. Not so: he or she desperately casts about for a first sentence and then hopes for the best. If told to begin by making an outline, the pupil is even more bewildered as to what to make it with.

The teacher should start out by getting the whole class to suggest ideas bearing on the topic, no matter how far-fetched; for that is how the writer's mind works. Next, show how they are sorted out, rejected, grouped, and subordinated according to some scheme. Outlining, if wanted, thus becomes a rational act, instead of a helpless groping in the dark. Finally, the teacher asks for the best idea with which to start the essay, and the best one to end it. This exercise may be repeated many times without in the least delaying achievement in actual writing. In fact, it may create a desire to get down on paper the fruits of this administrative preparation.

To reinforce results, the teacher of writing should also see to it that students speak as far as possible in complete and grammatical sentences. Not only is this helpful in business and the White House, it is a powerful aid to writing well with the least amount of revision: habit, habit, habit born of practice is the key to clear expression; and it is obviously absurd to demand "simple and direct" on paper and neglect the same in speech. That both demands are spurs to clear thinking is a free dividend.

But just as the teacher needs writing practice, so he or she may need the same in speaking. No use preaching and then giving a poor example. Here is a transcript from life: "The Boston Massacre, now—it wasn't a massacre, a riot, not even that—Okay? There was this crowd around the customhouse and the British sent soldiers—Okay? to see—a captain along was supposed to tell them—Okay? The crowd shouted 'Lobster!'—you don't see? That was on account the soldiers' red coats—Okay? Well, the captain said 'Don't fire'—Okay? but they were scared maybe and fired. They killed five—Okay?" By no means okay.

At the same time as the monitoring of speech goes on, firmly but kindly, so as not to hurt young sensibilities, enunciation can be attended to—clear vowels as well as clear thoughts. The value of this incidental training is not small. The modern world calls for tens of thousands of people whose job is to make announcements at microphones all day long. Very few do it well.

They mumble or drop their voice at the end of the sentence, which carries the important information; they call out an unusual name as briskly as if it were plain Jones or Smith; they speak at the same rate of speed as in face-to-face conversation, never suspecting that a crowd of people cannot hear properly unless "addressed," and not merely spoken to. As in bad writing, these faults betray thoughtless disregard of the party at the receiving end. Good speech, like good writing, is a form of civility.

Plainly, to read, and what to read, are questions that take one pretty far. This is due to the nature of the mind, where thought, word, and utterance form an endless chain. The school has apparently forgotten the connection and dropped the last link. The result is a second set of illiterates—the non-writers. For although in one sense Americans read a great deal (see below), they have delegated writing to specialists—the professionals whom we call Writers and those others, in advertising and public relations, who have come to be known, not surprisingly, as the "creative department."

Give Her a Book?
She *Has* a Book

. . . .

Columbia Magazine, December 1987

Among the groups that stand high on the list of National Worries are two very large ones: people who have got through high school and can't read and people who can read and have got through college but don't read. The former have long been the special concern of observers who are beginning to be believed and whose recommendations are being adopted.*

The other group about whom it is our duty to pray and do something has been courageously tackled by the [former] Librar-

---

*Tomorrow's Illiterates: The Present State of Reading Instruction Today, ed. by Charles C. Walcutt, Preface by Jacques Barzun, Little, Brown, Boston, 1961.

ian of Congress, Dr. Daniel Boorstin, who founded at his institution The Center for the Book. It holds conferences, sets up exhibits, and addresses exhortation and encouragement to all those suspected of being out of reading practice since they took off their mortarboard on that hot June afternoon.

The idea is to get them in trim again, like their counterparts whom the doctors urge to do a few push-ups or a little jogging every day. The habit would limber up their minds and do good to the book publishers at the same time. For the country produces more books every year—over 100 a day—for its 230 million inhabitants. But most print orders are for 5,000 copies, and a book is deemed a success (though its cost is hardly met) when it has to be reprinted and reaches 10,000 copies sold—one to every 23,000 people.

You may say, What about the book clubs? They do indeed get books into readers' hands—many more than would get distributed without clubs. But the limit of their propelling power is soon reached, on any level. I know this from first-hand experience, because during the 12 years that straddled the 1950s, I was part of a trio with Lionel Trilling and W. H. Auden that selected and reviewed books for a "quality" club. At its peak, the club had 40,000 members, and no promotion could push the figure higher. Our efforts did circulate more books of the solid kind—say four times the number that any one book would have reached unaided, or one book to every 5,000 of the population: tremendous!

These facts conceal a more complex situation. The millions of college graduates who are set down as non-readers are being unintentionally maligned. They do read; they read a great deal, but it is not what may be called hard reading. I do not mean that they only read trash. The opposite of "hard" is "soft"—printed matter that has escaped hard covers and quite often has no covers at all. Let me explain.

What printers and publishers of this nation relentlessly discharge at the reading public is a mass of important but fugitive material. There are, to begin with, a host of magazines of concern to every trade and profession, to every interest, sport, and hobby. They live and thrive in droves, as one can see when they change hands: CBS recently sold 21 of a kind in a single clutch. And new ones start up without cease, as groups define themselves by taste. People who collect bottle tops or want to do their own haircutting must be served, and are. What this means is that every month the alphabetically fit are offered a wad of articles and ads that equals a book in length. It has first claim on attention because it feeds an existing passion, because it offers variety in small, premasticated portions, and because it has been paid for ahead of time.

This payment, by the way, can be very small. One can get almost any magazine for eight months at a nominal "inducement price." Supposing a person of wide-ranging mind, he or she could satisfy the strongest reading appetite by going from one craft or sport to another endlessly—eight months at a time for a couple of dollars each.

Filling in the gaps between the specialist magazines, there are of course the political weeklies, the artistic and literary journals, and a sizable collection of academic quarterlies, all these on top of pure scholarly journals, numbered by the hundreds and proliferating too. Here should be added the societies which devote themselves to a single author—Jane Austen or Rex Stout—and of which there are said to be over 300: all publish regular bulletins.

Nor is this cornucopia of periodical literature more than one part of the output that confronts the college-educated day in and day out. If you own a couple of shares of stock in one or more corporations, you receive their annual and other reports, and I defy anyone who likes attractive printing, picturesque scenes, and superb photography to throw away all these documents unread. Though the subject matter is commonplace, they contain the best American prose now written—no academic jargon, journalese, or obscurantist nonsense. The ghosts who produce the statements by the chairman of the board and the heads of divisions want to be understood and to persuade. And next door to the harangues are vivid descriptions that go with the stunning four-color pictures: oil rigs in the Pacific, a hotel lobby in Denver, women assembling electronic pianos in Mexico, and heaven knows what other conglomerate activities happen to belong that year to Allied Trades Unlimited.

The stockholder large or small necessarily has a bank account, children or nieces and nephews at a private school, and something of a conscience. This typical set of features means that he or she is the target of the most abundant kind of soft reading matter. I refer to newsletters. The bank obviously cannot carry on its business without telling its customers with every batch of canceled checks how much better it performs than its competitors. The schools are of the same opinion about themselves and moreover must keep the parents haired up as to donations for teachers' salaries, while they show how the pupils are kept haired down by Mr. X in math and Mrs. Y in English. Their pictures, beaming, are there to prove it. Without the newsletter, parents would hardly remember that schools mean teachers and subjects, let alone salaries.

Finally, the now-overwhelmed reader takes a worthy interest in his town or neighborhood, in the local hospital, and in one or more general causes of national or international scope—the Boy Scouts, U.S. English, the Indian Youth Council, or the relief of some stricken region of the globe. Proponents of all these causes issue newsletters, some of which are as informative—and as gripping—as good contemporary history and sociology. They take their share of reading time, a larger share, perhaps, than the peruser thinks, for although he may contribute money but once a year, these educational reminders come five or six times as often.

The net result of this blizzard of printed sheets is: we all read a great deal, and most of it not at all frivolous reading. Add to it plain advertising—so-called junk mail—part of which gets itself read in spite of defensive self-training, and it is no wonder that a book has a hard time breaking through the print barrier.

Nevertheless, in talking with friends who are not academics, I have found that "the book" is not a forgotten entity. If anybody is ever in doubt about the thing itself, it was defined 35 years ago by UNESCO as "a non-periodical literary publication containing 49 or more pages, not counting the covers." So the book is easy to identify; one must only be careful not to count the covers. Anyhow, its look and feel are remembered from college days, often with pleasure and almost always with guilt. Dr. Boorstin sounding his desperate horn call, like Roland losing the fight against the infidels, is not unheeded by the literate host who read the things I have enumerated.

What some of them do to salve their conscience is to buy every so often a bunch of paperbacks. They are sought and treasured like the "indulgences" that brought on the Protestant Reformation—pardons bought with good money but not really earned. These paperbacks, for lack of time, go on the shelf unopened. And to be fair, one must add that a good many issues of the three or four magazines subscribed to also remain unread.

Again at times, the noise around a best-seller, a blockbuster bulging its cheap covers with clay-laden paper and undistinguished gray print, compels the conscientious to buy, and some—not all—to read. The book may be a good one; there is no law of man or nature against it. But most often the work is only a quick throwing together of news articles and interviews about a recent event—a scandal, an assassination, a crook's memoirs, a natural disaster; in short, it is soft stuff hiding in hard covers, a sheep (for once) in wolf's clothing.

That people want to read a second time and in excessive detail what they have already learned from the newspaper is a tribute to their habits of thorough study—or is it a sign of reading fatigue, a numbness brought on by the essential monotony of the annual report, the handyman magazine, and the ubiquitous newsletter?

It is this last, I have come to think, that has become the great menace, not just to the reading of books but to leisure, sanity and the pursuit of happiness. I confess to a touch of paranoia about it, which is but an effort to escape. At any rate, it matches the mania of producing publications about publications. Three journals that I enjoy and need for my work have long since thrown in a quarterly newsletter. Now the American Philosophical Society, which has always issued its *Proceedings* and *Transactions,* has superadded a newsletter. Two academic magazines that I occasionally see and that I do not want to embarrass by citing have just yielded to the same narcissism—another newsletter.

Photography and the wish to make sure of steady praise have a good deal to do with the fad. Everybody in an organization must get credit on top of salary and fringe benefits, for it has become a kind of virtue, a piece of saintliness, to do one's bread-earning work; so there must be a record of it in the form of a group picture, an award, a jolly citation published to the world. The *Encyclopaedia Britannica,* which issues several thick and useful annuals, sends out a glossy newsletter, and so do many other publishing firms.

If Gutenberg had thought of it in time, collectors of incunabula would now have not only the great Bible of 1456, but a broadsheet to go with the pair of fat books. It would show Johannes (in a woodcut) sitting casually on a stack of three sets, with his daughter Errata smiling on one side and his Italian foreman Malfolio on the other. The caption would explain the scene and descant on the glory of the printing press so as to make one believe it. Books, it would point out, do not grow out of the ground; they have to be heroically set up in type, which at our plant is done under the expert supervision of the master who, etc., with the invaluable help in proofreading of the two shown here with inky fingers and a complacent smirk.

Obviously, a publisher is easily tempted to double his public appearances in this way, but other institutions feel the same itch and pay handsomely for the pleasure of scratching it. As a trustee of a cooperative library in New York, I carry on a guerrilla war against recurrent proposals to bring out "something about our work." The bulletin that lists for our subscribers the new books on hand does not seem to sate the floating lust for telling the world. One more piece of mail won't hurt the citizenry already inured to the gross annual tonnage of unsolicited information. Nobody throws away *everything;* some of it remains on the coffee table and keeps "our name" before the public.

That is how it happens that very few organizations of any kind—business, artistic, educational—are found today uncomforted by some periodical outpouring, newsletterless. I fully expect that now we have got in touch, the Man in the Moon will shortly say to himself, "I run an old and respected institution; we have done good service over the years helping to keep the tides going up and down; I'd better start issuing a newsletter, *The Lunar Month,* to explain to our many well-wishers how things look from this vantage point."

After such an orgy of soft utterance, the wonder is that some of us continue to write books. Perhaps among the abler unem-

ployed a force could be recruited to read them. I would undertake
to edit a newsletter telling them both how and why.*

But let us return to "hard reading," that is, reading books in hard
covers, the hardness being supposed to imply a lasting quality in
the contents, or at least a fair amount of it. What do these covers
actually promise nowadays? Not long ago the editor of *Harper's*
declared: "Of the thousands of books published every year, almost
all (possibly as many as 95 in every 100) constitute little more
than puffed up essays or articles. The author could have said what
he had to say in 40 pages instead of 400." The appeal, moreover,
is neither to the cultivated mind, nor the sensitive ear, nor the
concrete imagination. Its very success depends on the reflex response to ready-made phrases. That is in a sense appropriate since
the subjects are the current crises, the lives of the well-known,
and the analysis of "conditions," with or without remedies attached. In a word, these books are not hard reading but journalism, much of it very able when judged by that standard, which
includes speed of production.

Where is the book that would be congenial to the educated
mind, a book really new and worth rereading? Someone wrote
it—one of the five out of the hundred; but the reviewers passed it
by in their search for the newsworthy; the bookstores cannot afford to stock it—it's not on a burning subject; nobody hears of it
except by chance. Even if noticed here and there, its "shelf life"
at the publishers' is officially six months, after which it is headed
for the pulping mill or the remainder house. That is part of the
answer to the question "Where?" Read the remainder catalogues
and buy sight unseen if you want to keep in touch with literature.

Do not misunderstand: literature as I use it here does not
mean only books destined for greatness, future classics, though
some may be. That does not matter now. Literature has many
mansions; the lesser genres have merit and keep their readers over
centuries. The literary art can be found in a crime story by Doro-
thy Sayers, a ghost story by M.R. James, a farce by Courteline,

*The section that follows is excerpted from "The Future of Reading Books," *Journal
of Communication*, Autumn 1978; reprinted in *Books in Our Future*, Library of Congress,
Washington, D. C., 1987. (Ed.)

or a poem by Ogden Nash. The seasoned reader allows himself a balanced diet and moves easily through the categories from Sophocles to Mr. Dooley, finding in each of them the literary thrill—the thrill of good words skillfully joined—on top of the wisdom of tragedy or the wisdom of humor.

And what of the reading-matter for the young—their textbooks and fun books? Bad or good influence begins there. Modern textbooks have long had a low rating; so low that McGuffey's *Readers* have been brought back into print, a kind of shaming operation. A competent observer calls the textbooks in use today "a disgrace. Badly written, factually sloppy, supremely boring, these books alone go a long way to undermining the very essence of education, a student's yearning to know more, to grow through reading."*

As for children's books and magazines, though a step up from their joint form in comic books, they either specialize in subjects of the adult kind—sports, mechanics, and so on—or they indoctrinate about the environment, sexual equality, divorce problems, and the like. The latest tells six-year-olds how AIDS may strike the family. The one periodical that pays attention to literary quality in its balanced and unpreachy offering is *Cricket*.

But of course most children do not read either the books or the magazines written for their entertainment; their only idea of reading comes from the schoolbooks thrust upon them in grade after grade; so that the dread of reading, the loathing for things in hard covers is well inculcated. No wonder that in addition to our army of functional illiterates there is a corps of experienced antiliterates. What can the Reading Recovery Project possibly do to save these minds in time? What motive would an intelligent child have to *recover* such reading?

While schoolbooks and the adult products evoke indifference or despair, the enthusiasm of manufacturers, librarians, and educationists for the imminent utopia-by-computer continues unabating. It is expected that those who will not crack a book will gladly gaze at the answer-laden screen. That may be, but if the shift occurs, it will amount to a conjuring trick; it will pass off something not literature—not even knowledge—for what belongs

*David H. Lynn in *Basic Education*, September, 1989.

under those names. The substitute in view so far is information, and predigested at that.

If you prompt the diskette to flash the names of the three musketeers, it will do so—indeed the names of the *four* heroes will appear. But no matter what it adds about them, you will have acquired no knowledge—neither of the characters, nor of the novel, nor of literature. Supposing a determined search for the real thing and the software available, it is hard to imagine who would prefer to sit for hours at a console clicking commands rather than in a chair turning a page.

Nor is the sleight-of-hand limited to the purely literary. Those who concede that books may survive but that teaching and research will soon rely largely on computers never question how the things they put in databanks and miscall knowledge will get there. Who will do the abstracting and organizing? the choosing of what to abstract to begin with? It is not unfair to add: Who among a generation of non-readers, poorly taught, insensitive to words, alienated from literature, and who assume that knowledge is an extension of the quiz program and the crossword puzzle could reinstate for the general public what they themselves have never been intimate with?

To do them justice, the programmers will work anxiously toward one kind of thoroughness. They will see to it that subscribers to the service can quickly settle an argument about the length of Brooklyn Bridge, whether in the regular or the metric system. The young researcher, too, will be able to get a full bibliography on the American Revolution. But in the end, the machine will subtly respond to our tendency to act *en masse,* not burning books perhaps, but burying them; not suppressing free speech, but in and out of school limiting the vocabulary; not censoring publication but turning over the choice of ideas to proxy pictographers. In short, reading books has all the going forces of culture against it. Young and old are deprived or deterred in one way or another from the pursuit of knowledge and pleasure, and it is no exaggeration to record the death of literature.*

* The last ten words were added after the publication of Professor Alvin Kernan's book *The Death of Literature* in September 1990. (Ed.)

10

Western Civ. or Western Sieve?

INTRODUCTORY

It might clear the air if the discussion of Whose Tradition?—the current battle of the books—began with a few facts. A while ago, a teacher in a high school near Washington was threatened with dismissal for teaching the classics, apparently to the great advantage and satisfaction of the students. At the other end of the country, in Oakland, California, where Mortimer Adler was explaining the Paideia proposal to include the classics in the high school curriculum,* the skeptical superintendent of schools challenged its feasibility. The upshot was the setting up of a seminar composed of students from several parts of town, of every social and ethnic background, and selected only for their willingness to read "hard books."

Dr. Adler led the discussions which bore on the great political documents of this country—Declaration, Constitution, Federalist Papers—together with Machiavelli's *Prince*. The success of the trial was complete. This is not a rumor or a report: video tapes are there to prove the fact. The students were so enthralled that they put together a scrapbook of tributes to the discussion leader, full of significant comments: they had never before been asked for their opinion on serious issues of politics and society; none had been held to logical, consecutive thought; all felt that the subjects taken up were relevant to their lives. All this implied that their differences of color and upbringing never occurred to them as obstacles to understanding, let alone as reasons for feeling offended by a concern with Western ideas. In their innocence

*The Paideia Proposal, Macmillan, New York, 1982.

128

they probably thought they were Americans and not Asians, Africans, or members of that long-extinct tribe, the Latins. If anybody there was a Latin, it was Machiavelli.

The current obscurantism which attacks the Western tradition with the zeal of censorship, comes not from those supposedly unrepresented in the curriculum, but from academics and other intellectuals who *are* represented and hate their own heritage. This rejection follows two parallel lines, one political, one social. Because American institutions fail to live up to their own (Western) ideals, this country is detestable—an unmitigated disaster. Therefore all that led up to it must be abhorred and discarded. Columbus is stigmatized. The white peoples are "the cancer of the human race." The young must be taught ideas and ideals produced anywhere but in the West. What is wanted is a decolonization of the intellect.

The other social animus springs from class feeling, also put on and promoted by members of a class other than the one supposedly making the demand—popular culture touted by the graduates of high culture. The latter is undemocratic, snobbish, the plaything of the few, in short elitist—what worse could be said of it? So for this reason too, the school program must change and take up simultaneously the ethnic and the popular in place of the highfalutin: "it no longer speaks to us." The yearning to include expresses itself by eagerness to exclude.

It is odd that it is the United States that has given birth to this doctrine and finds it warmly espoused by school systems and universities—our country, which was peopled and shaped by refugees who left Europe because they took literally the liberating words of the classical authors, from Luther, Calvin, and Wesley to Locke, Montesquieu, Rousseau, Fourier, and Tocqueville, and of course, the poets and novelists who infused theory with imagination.

One can understand how the already educated might be bored by repetition of the liberal and critical philosophy; but that the next generation should be denied it and taught foreign ones only remotely connected with things in our landscape, cannot be justified except as a means of destroying the present order.

Would it work? As a weapon, it could certainly foster cultural division and ultimately separatism, especially since those it seeks to "represent" are only a few of the many stocks that made or are making the country. But before it could do anything, the new foreign classics themselves would have to prove teachable. One would like to see the faces of the schoolboys and girls after assignments in the Analects of Confucius and the History of Ssu-ma Chi'en, the Upanishads and the Bhagavad Gita, the Mahabharata, the Pillow Book of Sei Shonagon, and the speeches of Mohammed.

The difficulties in these great works lie in both what is said and how it is said; for example, Arjuna goes by fourteen alternative names, Baharama by six others, and so on down the list of characters. But that is among the least of the hurdles. More troublesome is that many of the Eastern classics present chiefly religious doctrine, creation stories, and moral precepts: "In the Ariyana discipline, music is lamentation. In the Ariyana discipline, dancing is sheer madness. In the Ariyana discipline, laughing that displays the teeth is childishness. Wherefore, brethren, do ye break down the bridge that leads to music, dancing, and laughter." (From the sayings of the Buddha on Stability of Societies.)

Now it is true that the great books of every civilization are the voices of human experience and as such worth reading and pondering. But that experience and its expression are so modified by time and place and the whole past of the particular people that the experience is not accessible without long and arduous study. It is hard enough to get the meat out of the writings of one's own tradition. Where are the schoolteachers who would spend years mastering those of the Orient? They could manage but one at most since a knowledge of the language is essential. And what holds for philosophy and religion holds for history and fiction. Subject matter not being, these days, the strong point of teacher preparation, one wonders what will be taught as Oriental or other studies.

The second line of attack sounds more plausible: teach customary culture, not the classics. Forget books and discuss folkways and beliefs, the songs and festivals of the various groups that make up the United States. Think what a boost it would be to their self-esteem! No teaching of their ancestors' highbrow ideas could do as good a job: Chinese philosophy would not explain the Korean or Vietnamese or Cambodian emotions of today, or the many other kinds that deserve a place in this survey of the world. At the very least, the study of the living cultures of our ethnic groups would remove the appalling provincialism of the West. By extension, it would generate tolerance for all peoples that on earth do dwell, and it would certainly appeal—a picturesque, multi-colored, entertaining kind of social studies, and not hard work at all for teacher and taught.

A tempting prospect but for the fallacies in it. In the first place, it is a question whether school programs should be tailored to make this or that group feel honored. Cultural pride may be a good thing, clannish conceit is not; nor does it need school assignments in order to flourish. Second, tolerance—which runs counter to conceit—does not come from knowing how other people dance, worship, and get married. In Beirut, Christians are killing Christians, and Muslim, Muslim. They know only too well their enemies' customs. A common heritage did not prevent the War of 1812 with England or of the North and South in 1861.

Third, the provincialism of the West is a myth. It is the West, and not the East, that has penetrated into all parts of the globe. It is only the West that has studied, translated, and disseminated the thoughts, the histories, and the works of art of other civilizations, living and dead. By now, the formerly shut-in peoples do take an interest in others, but this recent development is in imitation of Western models. By good and bad means, Western ideas have imprinted themselves on the rest of the world, and one result is that cultural exchange and mutual instruction are at last consciously international; this, just at the time when we are told to repudiate our achievements and consign our best thoughts to oblivion.

How far this form of moral suicide will spread is unpredictable. One textbook publisher is bringing out a two-volume collection of *The Literature of the Western World,* so all is not lost: Western Civ. will last through 1991 and perhaps the following semester. But for those who do not want to see their heritage leak away through the present holes in the curriculum, it is important to be aware not solely of the contents of the classics, but also of their second pedagogic function: properly taught, they develop the ability to think.

For teaching the classics means grappling with momentous ideas and complex arguments—those found in the philosophy and theology, the political and social theory, the poetry, drama, and fiction that are called classical.

Students in seminars (as at Oakland under Mortimer Adler) are not merely to "give their ideas" in the raw state, but to read those in the text correctly, express them and their own cogently, and defend their choice against equally rational opposition from their fellows and from the instructor, who will act as devil's advocate. Only when students can do this can they be said to think—something radically different from the common utterance, "I think this is wrong" (dictatorship, capitalism, investment in South Africa, surrogate motherhood, and the rest).

It is no doubt utopian to imagine that the schools in their present state can turn to and use the classics in this way. But some good schools now in being and others that will reform themselves can make a beginning, while the colleges that have kept some notion of why they exist will surely hang on to the humanities in their original form, the great books in every genre. With luck, the result might be a generation that can think better than those leaders of opinion who out of unspent hatred are bent on war against the West.

Of What Use the
Classics Today?

St. John's College, July 17, 1987; St. John's College
Bulletin, September 1987; *Paideia Bulletin,*
October 1989; *Perspective,* Council for Basic Education,
Winter 1988–89

The first service that a classic does is to connect the past with the present by stirring up feelings akin to those that once moved human beings—people who were in part very much like ourselves and in part very unlike. That is an interesting experience in itself—as interesting as traveling to Tibet or studying the home life of the kangaroo. It is in fact travel, travel in time as well as in space.

But before going on with the other uses of the classics, we should perhaps ask, "What *is* a classic?" so that we may be sure that we are all thinking of the same thing. Many definitions have been given, which include such words as universal and permanent. I distrust what they imply. The merest reflection shows that a classic in one country is hardly known in another—therefore not universal. Certainly the classics of the Far East do not exist as such in the Western world. And the Far East begins in Russia where, for instance, Pushkin's *Eugen Onyegin* is a very great classic. How many people know it over here? Only specialists, like those who know the classics of India, China, and Japan. So much for universality. As for permanence, history is there to tell us that over the centuries the great writers change in value like the dollar or the pound. Who today thinks of Cicero as a tremendous literary figure? Yet he was the idol of the Renaissance. And where was John Donne before T. S. Eliot and his followers made him their master? Shakespeare himself was canonized only 150 years ago by the Romantic poets and critics.

So our first notion about a classic should be that it is a variable designation; it is applied, or can be applied, to works that possess a certain potential of classicality. And it follows that there is no set number of classics—not 100 or 1,000—no definitive list, even though today in the West a very small group of works have held their own for about 400 years. This is what has given the illusion of permanence. But there are thousands of works in many languages that are or could be treated as classics.

The question, then, shifts to what makes a work potentially a classic. Here one can point with more assurance to certain features. The first is "thickness," as Henry James called it, referring not to the width of the book on the shelf, but rather to the density of its discourse: much is going on in every line or paragraph; every sentence contains an idea; the whole work covers acres of thought and feeling; whereas the ordinary book, no matter how thick in physical measurement, pegs away at one or two little matters—anything from *How to Win Friends and Influence People* to any of the recent discussions of Japanese industry. Likewise, the poems and novels of our daily fare may be enjoyable or instructive, but they do not recast for us the whole world into a new shape. They throw a few glancing lights on what we already know or suspect.

A second mark of the classic might be called its adaptability. When first launched, it fits an existing situation, perhaps an existing demand. Homer's *Iliad* was doubtless in request by the descendants of the conquerors of Troy. It entertained and flattered them to hear the tale of past glory, not too far in the past. Or, jumping to a much later book and a different situation, the English Civil Wars prompted Hobbes to write *The Leviathan* as a guide to political action. The work suited neither side in the struggle, but that doesn't matter—it did fit the actual predicament, though partisans could not see it.

Today, that same work fits the recurring situation of nation-wide disorder and compels us to think not only about the nature of the state, but about the nature of man. For Hobbes begins with a short treatise on psychology. A classic's thickness makes it serve more than its original purpose. It is owing to this capacity that the classics come and go at different times. Shakespeare did not suit the Augustan age, because he was irregular, wild, ignorant of all that mattered to the Age of Reason. But to the Romanticists who came next, those very defects became great qualities, and Shakespeare was rapidly promoted a classic.

The successive situations that a classic must fit are not of the same kind: the first time it is usually the state of society at the

moment; later, it is probably the state of mind of artists and thinkers in search of what Coleridge called "elements that are wanted."
These elements, to be sure, have some relation to society, but it is
never the general public that digs out, or as we say, revives, the
neglected, half-forgotten classic.

This fact leads us to the third requisite that a classic must
have—another obvious one: it must gather to itself enough votes
to be openly, publicly *called* a classic. The number required is
indefinite, of course, and the vote is never unanimous. There is
always, about every classic, an unconvinced minority. For example, in each generation many scholars think Virgil's *Aeneid* a
feeble plagiarism of Homer, just as in the eighteenth century
many believed Homer a barbaric sketch that Virgil had wonder-
fully perfected. Today, there are plenty of people who think
Shakespeare is a mediocre playwright, beginning with the theater
people who produce him, since they cut, change, add, and generally spice up his plays with novelties before they let us see them
on the stage. But an opposition, no matter how large, is usually
silent.

One last point about classics: after a work or an author has
been voted in, it is the academic community that records the vote
and prolongs the term of office. Generally, one masterpiece is
chosen as *the classic* by the given author and it is made compulsory reading. Editions with notes and introductions are published
and thrust into the hands of the young, who suffer or not, depending on the teacher. In either case, the label is fixed in the minds of
the next generation: no doubt is possible: Shakespeare, Milton,
Keats; Homer, Virgil, Dante; Twain, Melville, Poe; Dickens,
Fielding, Swift are classics for the English-speaking world—today. By a further wrinkle, there is often a discrepancy between
academic and what is called critical opinion. In my youth, Dickens was still read in high school, but leading critics thought him
an inferior novelist. He has made a comeback, thanks to a few
critics, followed by most, but not all, of the others. The main
body is made up of sheep, led by a shepherd and a barking dog.

By now you are doubtless impatient to get to the further uses of
the classics, beyond the first one I mentioned, that of establishing
a live link with the past. To understand the next use required our

going into the nature of a classic, because this second use is: to teach how to read. I mean "read" in the honorific sense of read intelligently and thoroughly. Because a classic is thick and full, and because it arose out of a past situation, it is hard to read. The mental attitude and attention that are good enough for reading the newspaper and most books will not work. We read ordinary matter by running the eye over the print at a steady rate, rarely stopping to think or wonder. The material was chosen and written precisely for this rapid, effortless pace. The easy progress is habit-forming and that is why the overwhelming majority everywhere, including most of the college educated, read only contemporary books, and of these only the read-as-you-run. In college these people may have struggled with a handful of classics and escaped unaffected, but more probably the curriculum was adapted to their tastes, and the readings in English and American literature were of the current sort. Then, once a B.A.—goodbye to all that!

But why, after all, learn to read differently by tackling the classics? The answer is simple: in order to live in a wider world. Wider than that? Wider than the one that comes through the routine of our material lives and through the paper and the factual magazines—*Psychology Today, House and Garden, Sports Illustrated;* wider also than friends' and neighbors' plans and gossip; wider especially than one's business or profession. For nothing is more narrowing than one's own shop, and it grows ever more so as one bends the mind and energies to succeed. This is particularly true today, when each profession has become a cluster of specialties continually subdividing. A lawyer is not a jurist, he is a tax lawyer, or a dab at trusts and estates. The work itself is a struggle with a mass of jargon, conventions, and numbers that have no meaning outside the specialty. The whole modern world moves among systems and abstractions superimposed on reality, a vast make-believe, though its results are real enough in one's life if one does not know and follow these ever-shifting rules of the game.

Since it is a game and a make-believe, anybody who wants access to human life and its possibilities—to thoughts and feelings as they occur natively or by deep reflection—must use an-

136

other channel. One such channel can be cut by using the classics of literature and philosophy; a second can be made through the fine arts and music. I say "made" and "cut" not "found," because of that "thickness" to which I keep coming back. The great works do not yield their cargo on demand. But if one reads them with concentration (for one "reads" works of art, too), the effort gives us possession of a vast store of vicarious experience; we come face to face with the whole range of perception that mankind has attained and that is denied by our unavoidably artificial existence. Through this experience we escape from the prison cell, professional or business or suburban. It is like gaining a second life. Dr. Johnson, who was not given to exaggeration, said that the difference between a lettered man and an unlettered was the difference between the living and the dead.

This enlargement of vision has a useful by-product. The same habits of persistent scrutiny, of sensitivity to what is not said but implied, of patient meditation after encountering what is strange—all enhance the power of judging life situations and human character. A course of the classics does not guarantee that a person will be happier or more ethical, but it does foster a certain detachment that tends to make for serenity and possibly for greater decency.

In a still more practical, immediate way the classics serve human needs, because they are an extraordinary means of communication. At the lowest level they supply names and phrases charged with multiple meanings—shortcuts in explanation and persuasion; and at the highest, they create a means of mutual understanding based on what is an actively shared experience.

The first of these aids to communication comes from the fact that the classics have contributed to the general vocabulary, even though the ordinary citizen is not aware of it. Take a recent headline on the front page of the *New York Times:* "Aluminum Not the Achilles' Heel of the U.S.S. Stark." The reference was to the ship bombed in the Persian Gulf, and it was the first indication that the ship had a heel. Achilles' heel of course means weak spot, but the newsman preferred a colorful turn of phrase; he used it perhaps without knowing where it came from and how it got its meaning. Nor is this an isolated instance. In one issue of *Time*

137

magazine I found: The Golden Mean, a judgment of Solomon, and crossing the Rubicon. People evidently think by means of these images, and there are fat reference books to tell the ignorant what they stand for. Taken together, they might be described as the fall-out from the high energy of the classics.

Now it would seem desirable to know these things in their original setting, in context. Especially now that education is skimpy, these traditional allusions are being corrupted by misuse and therefore lost to clear meaning. One comes across such things as: "undo the Gordon knot" (presumably a splice invented by one Gordon); the "rock of Sillyphus," and "a Senatorian shout." As for King Canute, that very intelligent ruler is misrepresented as wanting to roll back the ocean, when in fact he was showing his courtiers that he could not stem the tide (of events) as they apparently wanted. In short, if one likes to know what one is talking about, it is well to be acquainted with the stories that give point to the catchwords.

And when one goes from the newspaper to ordinary books on contemporary matters, one will be at a loss if unable to grasp what is implied by quotations from the great poets, philosophers, and novelists. Authors find it a convenient shorthand to write: the thing-in-itself, more honored in the breach, Socratic irony, King Charles's head, Gargantuan appetite, mute inglorious Miltons— you can continue the list for yourselves. But again, reader and writer must be at one. Not long ago, I read an interview in which the wealthy builder of a new mansion said that he and his wife had now realized their dream of having "a fine and private place." What he did *not* "realize" was that he was quoting Andrew Marvell's description of the grave.

These classic elements of reading and writing are part of something larger known as our cultural heritage—the accumulated lore about our forebears, their doings and sayings. Nobody grows up in a settled society without picking up bits and pieces of it and being in some way molded by them. Young Washington and the cherry tree; Lincoln's log cabin and his toil as a rail splitter; General Sherman with his "War is hell" are fragments of past life embedded in the American mind. Their use is not immediately apparent, yet they mean more than "Do not tell a lie"; "humble origins do not keep a good man down," and so on. They recall a scene and carry a deeper message than the platitude they express: Sherman's emphatic word comes not from a pacifist but from the man who led a march of devastation into the South. It is this half-expressed, half-implied part that does the work of cultural continuity and keeps a nation unified thanks to common feelings and common understanding.

A famous anecdote makes the point. The poet Coleridge was once lecturing in London about English literature and happened to mention that Dr. Johnson, coming home one night, found a woman of the streets who had fainted from hunger and lay in the road. He picked her up and carried her on his back to his lodging, where he revived and fed her and housed her until she was well. Coleridge's fashionable audience snickered and clucked, the men amused, the women shocked. Coleridge stopped and said gravely: "I remind you of the parable of the Good Samaritan." Ten quick words settled the murmuring. The appeal to a common cultural example, in this case from the Scriptures, had dispelled foolishness and made the crowd think and feel as one. An hour's preaching about charitableness and the virtue of forgetting conventions when human life is at stake would have had no such decisive force; it would have been explanation and apology, whereas the allusion to the Bible instantly evoked the right emotions in harness with the right ideas.

I need not point out that the Bible was once among the compulsory classics that everybody learned to read and understand, in Sunday School first, and with refresher lessons during every sermon in church. This powerful bond of poetry, drama, maxims, historic figures and events, we have lost. Some of the phrases and names remain in use—*Time* magazine had heard of Solomon— but the force and frequency of reference grows weaker and the context grows thinner all the time; indeed, for millions of people in what used to be Christendom it has disappeared altogether. Just last month, the Metropolitan section of the *New York Times* quoted a conversation overheard on a bus between a young man and his girl companion. He was telling her about Jesus and his disciples, about the Last Supper, and the betrayal by Judas and his suicide by hanging. She was spellbound and kept interjecting: "Really?"

"You don't mean it!" "No kidding!" She had caught up at last with a classic thriller.

The need for a body of common knowledge and common reference does not disappear when a society is largely pluralistic, as ours has become. On the contrary, it grows more necessary, so that people of different origins and occupation may quickly find familiar ground and, as we say, speak a common language. It not only saves time and embarrassment, but it also ensures a kind of mutual confidence and good will. One is not addressing an alien, blank as a stone wall, but a responsive creature whose mind is filled with the same images, memories, and vocabulary as oneself. Since the Biblical source of those common elements can no longer be relied on, the other classics, the secular scriptures, remain the one means of creating a community of minds, a culture—indeed, a society in the original sense of the word, which is: a group of companions.

Otherwise, with the unstoppable march of specialization, the individual mind is doomed to solitude and the individual heart to drying up. The mechanical devices that supposedly bring us together—television and the press, the telephone and the computer network—do so on a level and in a manner that are anything but nourishing to the spirit. Even the highbrow programs on television present literature and history in garbled forms; the medium requires that costume, scenery, and moving vehicles upstage philosophy. What is worth noting is that the public seems to be vaguely aware of this great void: programs high and low are falling in popularity and the suppliers are worried.

From one who feels deprived in this way, recourse to the classics requires nothing new; it does not call for superhuman powers. To earlier generations, books were as natural a source of information and entertainment as broadcasts are to the young today. It was the urge to learn from books that made the common people clamor for education; they were willing to pay for public schools so that everybody could read and write. Rising in the world was a strong motive, but the satisfaction of curiosity about life was another. William Dean Howells tells us in his autobiography how people felt about books in his native town on the Ohio

140

around 1840. The river steamer would come up to the pier every so often—nobody knew exactly when—and amid goods of all kinds would unload a barrel of books. Within a few minutes of landing, these books would have been sold. The buyers were farmers and small tradesmen who had never been to high school, let alone college. Howells's self-education, like Lincoln's, came from these books.

Today, by contrast, the appetite for books has atrophied. It has to be promoted by our strongest agency—advertising. The book clubs shout themselves hoarse; the Library of Congress holds conferences urging the people to read a book—a real book, not a magazine devoted to a hobby, a sport, or a home industry. And now that the high school has caved in to the students' demand for visual treats, some colleges try hard to inoculate freshmen with a taste for habitual reading by offering or requiring courses in the humanities.

The question is, which books? What constitutes today the cultural heritage, which formerly was automatically taken as known by people who were educated and who educated others? The quandary is real, because of the large number of classics piled up during the last 500 years; and because the study of the languages needed to read the ancients has virtually ceased. Being troubled by this uncertainty, three thoughtful and learned persons have recently drawn up an inventory of nearly 5,000 facts, names, ideas, and technical terms required for "cultural literacy." That is their name for the minimum portion of the heritage they think adequate to maintain a national culture.

Having made and published the list, they are now at work on a dictionary that will explain the 5,000 terms. This double effort is praiseworthy; it should call attention to the spread of a damaging ignorance. But the remedy seems more mechanical than educative. To learn "the facts" about Aristotle and Luther and Alexander Hamilton and 4,997 others, all in the air, so to speak, would be a gigantic feat of memorization, whereas to learn these facts and much else while studying history and reading the classics is by comparison very easy. The facts then stick in the mind like the names of the streets around your house: you never set out to learn them, they come as part of your direct acquaintance with the place. This difference seems to me all-important; and it points to another use of the classics: they educate you as you read— provided you read them in the right manner and at the right time. Consider this last condition: when and how should the classics enter our lives? I have said that the classics cannot be read like a magazine article. It takes some form of compulsion to get started, and often the eager starter bogs down in difficulties. To give help, therefore, and to apply the steady pressure, coaching is necessary. Hence the classics must be met and conquered at latest in college.

At latest: the really appropriate time would be the last two years of high school, when the onset of maturing stirs feelings and thoughts about the meaning of life and the nature of society. Our obtuse educational experts would be astonished to see how passionately a group of perfectly average fifteen-year-olds can be brought to discuss Machiavelli's *Prince* or the *Confessions of St. Augustine*. But the opportunity is missed, and college offers the last chance of initiating the habit of reading and enjoying solid books.

The pressure or compulsion I speak of is best applied in the shape of a course required of all undergraduates and taught by members of any and every department, not by specialists in rotation—one man for the Greeks, another for the Middle Ages, and so on. For the sleepiest student can figure out that if reading all these books is declared good and necessary for all freshmen, it cannot be deemed bad and beyond the power of any teacher, even if he or she has been corrupted by years of research. And he or she must not merely teach the books, but show through speech and demeanor the effects of familiar intercourse with the classics. These must be seen to be used in daily life like food, clothing, and shelter.

Nor is a dip in freshman year sufficient. In every subject there are classics that are worth getting to know; in the social and physical sciences, too, where progress is supposed to have made classic works obsolete: the very nature of the errors is instructive, being part of the spectacle of original thought.

At the same time, I doubt the advisability of a curriculum entirely made up of great books. I will make up for what must seem a heresy in this college* by stating a principle I have evolved on my own and that you may find congenial: I believe that for the best results a college should be independent of a university, physically and administratively. Why? Because I think it essential for the undergraduate to live in the persuasion that what he is learning is of the highest importance—none higher—and that what he is acquiring is the most valuable of his future possessions. He is not just "qualifying," earning grades to gain entry into some other place closer to the "real world," after which he can forget all that preliminary stuff. The real world is what he carries on his shoulders, and his present business as an undergraduate is to create there a Self he can live with.

To make this set of beliefs secure, there must be no distracting, competing interests of the same intellectual order—or that look the same. Now a university is by definition a conglomerate of such interests. Hearing about them every day cannot help distracting: the clash of rival specialties, the endless comings and goings of professional people, the buzz of news and rumor defeat single-minded aims. To know this you need only talk to a provost or vice president for academic affairs: the business school is doing very well with its new computers, but the engineers can't seem to get a new dean. The liberal arts—well, they're in decline as usual. Everybody loves them, and the English department is still the biggest, but Greek and Latin have to divide one student between them. Meanwhile, the medical school is sulking—they want more money, more nurses, more bandaids. Not so journalism—I mean communication arts: *there's* the ideal school; it doesn't cost much to run and it has the largest registration ever; a perfect army of C-minus hustlers, with a few brilliant minds who will shape our opinions later on.

Such is a university—a Ferris wheel with some compartments always going up while others go down—no stability and a restless attitude toward college teaching and what should be taught. A separate college is a more graspable entity and it can stick to the meaning contained in the etymology of its name. Col-

*The St. John's College curriculum consists exclusively in the study of classic works in each field. (Ed.)

lege means persons chosen or brought together for a stated purpose. It is interesting to note that this same idea occurs in the Latin
word for reading and understanding: the eye *collects*—brings together—the letters and the meanings.

A college where the classics as well as the students are collected for a single purpose is thus free of the floating temptations
that pervade the university. I have mentioned one of these, the
notion of the "real world," represented on campus by law, business, and the other professions. Another is the idea of relevance,
confused as it is with the feeling of immediacy—whence it follows that the old classic books may be dispensed with. Relevance
is indeed a true standard of judgment, but it does not stand by
itself; it expresses a relation to something else—relevance to
what? for whom? at what point? If the classics are assimilated as
a furnishing of the mind-and-heart, a formative element in building up the Self, then the classics are relevant to that Self for an
entire lifetime, even though on a given day there is nothing in the
paper about the *Ethics* of Spinoza or *The Scarlet Letter.* To trained
readers both these works have a bearing on things the morning
paper does contain. Without conscious effort such readers make
use of the relevant parts in judging whatever they encounter. In so
doing they dispose of another illusion bred by university research,
the idea of the obsolete, the apparent elimination of the past by
the future, the belief propagated by science and industry that later
is better, even when later has not yet come about and is only a
prophecy by enthusiasts with something to sell.

Having so far sketched the advantages to be derived from the classics—their enlargement of the spirit by varied experience; their
use as a medium of rapid communication; their influence in building a Self and in strengthening the judgment—I am bound before
closing to add a word of caution. Like all good things, the classics
can be misused and lead to things that are the reverse of desirable.

Studying the classics can wind up in mere bookishness.
Their contents will have been absorbed faithfully and accurately,
but the mind that holds them seems unable to get outside its ac-
quisition and use it. If this is not due to an incurable flaw of the

mind, it is due to teaching that has trained perception and left out imagination. By imagination I do not mean undirected fancy or daydreaming. I mean imagining the real, making a successful effort to reconstruct from words on a page what past lives, circumstances, and feelings were like. This ability does not come to everybody by nature, yet any germ of it can be developed by practice after teaching has shown the way. It is anything but unchecked speculation. To imagine—say—the life of a medieval serf, one's ideas must conform to a large number of facts found in the sources, as well as catch somehow an impalpable atmosphere. Usually, one must first unlearn the many thought-clichés absorbed from miscellaneous reading, bad films, and cheap romances.

Imaginative understanding is what enables the mind to transfer its knowledge to new situations. The England of *Tom Jones,* the Russia of *War and Peace* are gone, but the tribulations of Tom and of Pierre can still serve as touchstones in the present, provided our imagination clearly sees how the growth of a young soul has been changed by a changed state of society and how it has remained the same.

Again, for this play of the imagination the works themselves must be read and read whole, not the summaries in reference books. Only at this price can the mind form true and distinct images. If, for example, one goes to essays or handbooks on "The Legacy of Greece," Homer, Plato, Thucydides, and the rest merge into an idyllic picture of a joyful pagan people, all connoisseurs of fine art and expert mathematicians. The developed imagination rejects such a picture at sight. It knows that these things cannot be, because it has acquired the power of seeing the world in three dimensions—fact, connotation, and general truth or probability. The mind does not get stuck in the first or second position.

To develop in the young this power to move freely among perceptions, teachers must exhibit it themselves. They must of course know how to prevent misconceptions and how to coax and cheer the weaker spirits over the hurdles. But if they happen to be specialists, they must not abandon the readings to teach the scholarship that relates to them. Nicholas Murray Butler, the president of Columbia University in my time, once told me of his taking when in college a course in Greek drama. On the first day, the instructor assigned a play of Euripides and said: "Gentlemen: this is the most interesting play by this author: it contains every one of the irregularities in Greek grammar."

One must be fair to the old scholar. From his point of view, it *was* the most interesting play. He was interested in grammar, not in plays, and certainly not in the classics as humanities. The confusion among these several legitimate aims explains the perpetual worry about the humanities in our colleges. A recent article tells us that among some academics there is disillusion about the value of the liberal arts. That is almost certainly an unintentional misstatement; the disillusion is—and ought to be—about presenting the liberal arts as if every student intended to become a scholar.

The same error has beset the professional schools, especially engineering and medicine. For fifty years I have heard their spokesmen bemoaning the lack of general intelligence in their students. Every few years these schools have another go at a liberal arts requirement—so many courses and lectures: it does not work, and the naive wonder recurs as the professionals compare their great men of 1900 with the stunted types of today. You cannot make humanists by courses *about* the humanities; they must be courses *in* the humanities, taught by humanists.

In the humanist mode there are no barriers between ideas, there is no jargon, no prevailing theory or method. There are books and readers, as on the first day of publication. Some of the results of scholarship may be brought in to shed occasional light on and around the work, but the work is there to shed its own light; it is not material for dissection or dissertation. Well read, everything in it may be usefully related to the world and to the Self; it is the role of the imagination to forge the links. No doubt there are dangers in this free realm as in every other. It is easy to talk nonsense and make false connections. But the reward of reading with a humanistic eye is not in doubt: it is pleasure, renewable at will. That pleasure is the ultimate use of the classics. All the great judges of human existence have said so, from Milton who called reading "conversation with the master spirits" to Virginia

Woolf, who imagined the Almighty saying to St. Peter about some newcomers to heaven: "Look, these need no reward. We have nothing to give them . . . They have loved reading."

I can only add one thing: it is always time to stop repeating the wise sayings and begin to believe them.

ADVANCED
WORK

11

Why Go to College?

To the incoming freshman, college used to be a revelation—of freedom, of his own maturity, of high seriousness in things of the mind. In most cases the boy or girl had never been away from home and was now alone responsible for the use of time and resources, no longer pupil but student. He or she was called Mr. or Miss in class, without irony. The whole intellectual landscape was new: here were grave faculty members, friendly but not chummy, devoting a good many hours a week to teaching certain definite matters of agreed importance and also doing that mysterious thing "research." It seemed to give their words the authority they claimed and did not hesitate to exercise. This enchanting new atmosphere found its counterpart in the work to be done—many hours of reading in real books, written by adults for adults, who were deemed capable of understanding all the words and of singling out the important points to remember.

This description of the step up from high school as it was fifty years ago has lost all validity. The college—and the university around it—have been transformed into a motley social organism dedicated to the full life. It does include the mental life, but certainly makes no fetish of it. Rather, intellect weaves in and out of the main business, which is socialization, entertainment, political activism, and the struggle to get high grades so as to qualify for future employment.

The new college is of this kind because incoming freshmen have long since achieved their freedom; they have known for years—parents, counselors, and advertisers told them so—that

151

they are mature and entitled to endless options, mental and physical; they are experienced in money matters, practiced in sex, and
blasé about studies. The last two years of high school have offered
courses nominally like those once required of college freshmen,
and "research" holds no mystery: they have been expert at it since
the seventh grade.

Everything else in the university has changed in parallel.
The faculty does not see teaching as its principal task nor does it
find any particular body of knowledge necessary for the degree.
Its members look upon the institution as a convenience for their
own ambitions, whose fulfillment lies outside the gates. If moved
at all by loyalty, the professor directs it to his fellow specialists,
to his source of funds—government agency, industry, or foundation—and possibly to one or two favored students who will follow
in his wake.

This turning of the academic effort from inside to outside
has made university governance difficult at the same time as it has
transformed central administration into a bureaucracy—internal
services and external relations demand it. The sprawling, anony-
mous crowd replacing the self-governed "company of scholars" is
enough by itself to discourage institutional loyalty and to make
teaching a chore instead of a calling. Attempts to counteract this
downgrading by giving "Great Teacher Awards" only underscore
the fact: great teacher now means simply "teacher"—rare bird.

It is but fair to add that part of the distaste for teaching is a
result of the students' lack of preparation. They are bright and
willing, they have ideas, but they seem to know nothing firmly
and nothing alike. Many, far too many, cannot read, write, count,
think, or talk acceptably. Remedial courses take care of the worst;
the rest, unrewarding to deal with, are ignored or else helped
along by some philanthropic instructor in one or another subject,
who left-handedly tries to patch up the failures of the past.

For these failures the high academic profession must bear a
large part of the blame. For generations the proud professors have
refused to have anything to do with elementary and secondary
schooling—except to criticize it on their own hearthrug. They
scorn mere teachers without knowing any; they do not review
textbooks below the freshman level; they despise—instead of re-

forming—the department of education in their own university. In other countries all recognize that teaching has equal importance and merit at every rung of the ladder. The most highly trained scholars begin by teaching in the *lycée* or *gymnasium* or the English "public" and "grammar" schools.

In the United States, college and university are undergoing the fitting punishment of their snobbish neglect: all the ills of the lower schools have infected the higher—bureaucratic rules and paperwork; students incapable and beyond rescue, but promoted yearly; a curriculum without plan or direction; subject matter dictated by politics or current events. Tailored to youthful tastes, such courses lack order and substance—invertebrate data in place of "disciplines." Around these attractions the campus re-creates the whole of society: unions and strikes, protests, insults, violence, madness, and the agencies needed to cope with these diversions. There must be a small army of security guards, a corps of psychiatrists and counselors, facilities for free artistic productions, a supply of contraceptive information and devices, and housing and subsidies for political and ethnic separatism.

It is no wonder that tuition costs have soared. The campus has become a large village or small town committed to giving full social services. And no wonder, again, that to meet costs it must admit students visibly unfit, and to obtain these, advertise its wares in the language of trade. "To Expect the Best, To Achieve the Best, Come To———" Or: "Successful But Not Satisfied? A Graduate Degree Can Make a Big Difference." Madison Avenue obviously sets the tone when in a full-page ad by one of the half-dozen leading universities a sampling of subjects is grouped by kinds, and "Dutch Painting of the Renaissance" appears under the heading "Esoteric."

Of course, the pretence of higher learning continues amid the hurly burly, the sports corruption and scandals, and the bally-hoo of fund-raising. But as was asked by the head of a department in a large state university, not a nostalgic elder, but a ranking scholar in mid-career: "Sitting on my desk is a four-volume institutional self-study filled with charts, figures, 'mission statements' and the paper from half a forest, but nothing about education except jargon and platitudes. Where have we gone wrong?"

This state of affairs raises two related questions: Should we return to the ivory-tower university? And: What do the young go to college for? Begin with the second. The American people decided a good while ago that it wanted to ape the Chinese Empire and set up a Mandarin system. A college degree is required for any well-paid job in business, as well as for government service and the professions. The popular propaganda in favor of heading for college is supported by the latest statistics, which show that the gap between college-graduate salaries and the rest is widening.

"Mandarin" is here a courtesy word, for it hardly matters what the bachelor's degree is worth intellectually. The name college is magic by itself. Colleges abound and there is no assurance that the graduate from any of them knows anything in particular or knows it well. Mingling for four years in miscellaneous classrooms with a loosely selected group of boys and girls from other parts has value, and the usual extra-curricular activities may well "educate" in the worldly sense. But is it worth the crushing costs and the grand apparatus of scholars and deans and publications and curriculum committees?

Higher education, advanced work, was meant to do more than confer the advantages just cited. Its task as defined by the great institutions was to put the next generation in possession of the social, political, and cultural heritage of the world. That heritage is not a secret formula; it allows some latitude in the choice of elements, but there is a core, defined by long reflection and practicability. It has been replaced by an offering that permits getting the degree with four years of freshman work, including Cinema Studies or Sexuality in Literature. Details of a serious-minded program are out of place here, but it is a sign that the needful criteria have been lost when we learn that 40% of college graduates have taken no history course and 77% no foreign language. To offset this vacuum, there are across the country 200 courses in "The Male Experience."

But was the ivory tower of any real use in a world which changes so rapidly? which is increasingly democratic, which— fill in your own cliché about what the world is like and is heading toward. Ivory tower is a question-begging phrase; its suggestion of dreamland is absurd. The men and women who made the American university a great institution were neither innocent nor aloof. They lived in the big world like the rest of the population. They had houses with mortgages attached; they had spouses and children and shared the hopes, fears, and ambitions that go with family life and professional work. And their concentration on learning and teaching enabled them to train young minds for the thoughtful life as well as the world's work.

That concentration by both parties to the venture is what requires calm surroundings and some distance from the tumult of real life, so-called. After all, the scientists working in Bell Labs shut the door on street fights, itinerant salesmen, and stump speakers. What goes on indoors is none the less real—and so are the activities of an "ivory-tower" university.

For the young, living in that fruitful oasis was of immense value. Even at an average institution it afforded four years of guided reflection on all aspects of life—reflection, not amateurish attempts at coping with global issues. It is false to suppose that something must be experienced before it can be known. Studying the theoretical developed the "imagination of the real," which is the basis of all practicality. The passage from youth to man- and womanhood, which embraces the choice of career, the sift among the uncertainties of mating, the substitution of individual for crowd-imposed tastes—all this was made a gradual accomplishment. Time and quiet permitted comparison and change of mind without penalty. It increased the chances of rational thought, decreased those of false starts, of regrets and the pain of late reversals of course.

Looking back, one can see how the world events of the 1940s and 50s first stunned the institutions of higher learning, halting them in their course, and then twisted them out of shape. The accident could not be helped; but the real misfortune was that motives of a low order kept those who knew what the idea of a university was from recovering it after the disarray.

The University
as the Beloved Republic

. . . .

Conference on "The University in America," Center
for the Study of Democratic Institutions, Los Angeles,
May 10, 1966; *The Center Diary,* September–October
1966; *The Center Magazine,* September 1969

Everybody knows what has happened to the university as an
institution since the Second World War. It has moved from
wherever it was to the center of the market-place. Through
its individual members as well as through its official undertakings,
it has come to take a direct part in the work of government, industry, and foreign affairs. Because of the rising population and its
rising demands for higher education, because of the lengthening
and thickening of professional training, the university, public or
private, has taken on the task of fitting the ambitions of young and
old to the needs of the day, these needs being defined in worldly
terms. Higher education is now supposed to lead straight into
practical life. In a word, the university is now a place for making
useful instruments, and both the institution and the world keep
telling each other that the future of the country depends on such
production being maintained. Self-congratulation about this new
importance exists on the campus, and a subtle flattery arises from
the new connection in the minds of businessmen and civil servants. The studious and abstracted air of the scholar is now the
preoccupied one of the man catching a plane and administering a
quarter-million-dollar grant.

There would be no need to review these familiar facts if they
did not constitute one half of a strange situation: for side by side
with this general exaltation at the university's fulfilling a high
practical role—a role being played by people once thought the
very cream of unpracticality—another emotion, another demand,
is at work, which is turning the university into something other
than its traditional self. What to call that something else is difficult, for there is nothing in our experience quite like it. Certainly

156

it is not the Church as we know it in modern times. Perhaps it is the Church as it was in the late, troubled empire of St. Augustine's day. All things considered, I tend to think that the nearest equivalent to what the university is becoming is the medieval guild, which undertook to do everything for the town. It dictated commercial fair play; it dispensed charity to the poor, sick, and aged; it gave feasts and plays and religious processions; it supported and supervised schooling, kept up roads and bridges, bargained with the overlords, and helped govern the borough. It also designed and repaired the town walls and manned them in wartime. This all-mothering activity is what made it the central institution of the town, the natural focus of the civic emotions, as well as the refuge of the afflicted.

So, when I hear the modern appeals to the university, appeals for immediate, direct public service to the community, appeals from undeveloped countries for talent, for exchanges of books and knowledge, appeals from government bureaus for experts and consultants on ever-longer leases—maybe I should say leashes—appeals from newspapers, radio networks, business concerns, and citizens at large: for advice, for information, for free tuition, for advanced seminars, and for choice artistic performances at no cost, I detect in all these requests not so much an expression of natural greed as a pathetic desire for light and love. The only thing that the guild used to provide and we do not is Masses for the dead, and if we do not it is because we are not asked.

The students, of course, want the appropriate counterpart of this full life. They want education for their souls, training for life, organized social and artistic activities, psychiatric help, and career planning and placement. The alumni want athletic spectacles (victorious for their side) and life-long flattery from the leaders of the institution that once was home.

But even this combination of all-purpose sanctuary and Delphic Oracle does not fully define the new relation of the university to modern society. In addition to all the public demands with which it is bombarded, the university receives more and more often the confessions of worldly men just past middle age, who want to give up their life of self-seeking in business or public

157

affairs, manufacture or advertising, so as to devote the remaining ten to fifteen years of their activity to the good works of a philanthropic institution, preferably a university.

These men express an unsatisfied longing for calm thought and high-minded, ill-requited reflection which they imagine prevails on the campus. They want to read a book they do not really like—as they once did; they generally make it clear that they have a practical shrewdness and talent for organization that the university could well profit from; and as they go on disclosing their vision I am left wondering whether there is the beginning of a monastic movement, the impulse of retreat being coupled with a utopian desire for perfect cooperation and ultimate companionship—in short, love, the beloved republic. In this mood of world renunciation the extremes join and businessman and beatnik, Madison Avenue and Big Sur move away from the bustling world, if not arm in arm at least in the same alienated step.

It is painful to disillusion these seekers from business and government. They are of course first cousins to the demanders of help and service who have destroyed the cloistered peace that these others hope to find. And I am not sure that the two kinds of clinging to Alma Mater's skirts are not fundamentally alike. To put it differently, I see in the transformation of the university the sign of a great social change that we have hardly begun to chart. A strong sense of it has informed some of the remarks at this conference, one speaker investing his whole moral capital in the academy as the sole and strict trustee of Western civilization, another wanting in modern society a self-perpetuating company of active and independent minds.

Why is the university the target for so many projects? I should be willing to answer by a play on words and say that these proposals, these projects, are projections—of hope and desire: a hope and a desire for a kind of place, a kind of connection, a kind of life, that our civilization no longer supplies, a place of disinterestedness, a life of contemplation.

Just compare what we know as the university today with what a university was as recently as seventy-five years ago. Here are the words of a guide to Oxford written in 1892: "Occasionally you will find among England's captains of industry one who has been at the University, and he will be proud of, and have profited by, his connection. But as a rule, the wealthy manufacturer does not send his son to Oxford. It is most unfortunate that the University has the reputation of unfitting a man for practical life, but it is deserved at least in part." Nowadays, it is not only expected, but acknowledged, that only the university will fit men for life in every profession, including business. The Oxford guide, in regretting the University's state and look of unpracticality, stood at the threshold of a new day, in which we, having redesigned the university for these heavily practical purposes, having pulled it into the midstream of business and professional life, now turn around and say longingly, "Where are those darling absent-minded professors?"

They were absent-minded, as William James finely said, because they were present-minded somewhere else. And it is that somewhere else that the whole world is looking for. How explain otherwise the passionate cry for creativity and freedom, the madness for the arts, the arts, especially the mad modern arts? I need not add that the feverish state of mind that I speak of is not restricted to unhappy businessmen and disillusioned civil servants. It prevails in everyone in and around the university. That is why there is so much agitation about academic freedom on the part of men who stand in no danger of political or religious censorship. What they look for under the name of academic freedom is a broad independence which society denies.

Similarly, the students are rebels, demi-rebels most of them, and fugitives from the world in the effort to discover what they call "life"—and they want it a fine life, a good life. This is their aim, surely, when they concern themselves with such affairs as war or urban renewal. They are against war, they are against urban renewal, they fight generously for civil rights, because these protests are another way of breaching the ordered world. Nor is the impulse limited to students. The divorce between "life" and the world, between what anyone would deem good and what society does, seems to thousands of thoughtful persons just a plain matter of fact. This assumption, if anything, is the radical split in our culture. What we suffer from is not the supposed breach between C. P. Snow's two cultures; rather, it is St. Augustine's per-

159

ception of the two cities: the city of the world and the city of God, forever irreconcilable.

If I may hazard a judgment which I hope is historically sound, I would say that these are the troubles of men who, coming at the ravelled end of Liberalism, have lost their religion, neglected their duties toward the State, and muddled art and charity and education into one indigestible mess. But that is a comment by the way. Our business here is to ask in all this, "What of the university? Is it thriving? Is it on the right road?"

Putting these questions to myself, I regretfully conclude that despite the clear advantages of an *intercursus magnus* between the university and men of affairs, when each sensible enterprise is judged separately, the sum total yields adverse results. I should like to mention a few of them without being accused either of starting a crusade or of touching the sacred clock—the one that nobody must ever appear to turn back, even when it strikes 13. Staying, then, within the limits of my assignment, which was to furnish hints toward an understanding of the university in modern society, I would venture three tentative conclusions:

First, making the university more worldly has enormously increased the power of professionalism, both inside and outside the university. The Mandarin system is now in the saddle everywhere, and with all its usual features: vanity, greed, faddishness, and punishment for the naive, who are often the geniuses. The contemporary spectacle of the curb market in prestige, with its bargains and bribes and daily ranking of men on the big board, is a reproach to intellect; and the goal of public service, which frequently leads to genteel prostitution in the halls of industry and charitable foundations, is no less a reproach to morality. We keep speaking of a company of scholars, but what we have in our new Babylons of higher learning is a scrimmage of self-seeking individuals and teams, the rugged age of gilded research. This commercial outlook, reinforcing professionalism, explains the absence of original ideas in almost every field of learning and will insure the continuance of that dearth for as long as the boom lasts.

Second, making research profitable and ecumenical has brought about a damaging shrinkage of time within the university.

Time now flows there at the same rate as outside, which accounts for the pressure and strain that every academic denizen groans under, while he also feels balked by the manifest futility of much of what he does. It does not in fact take a tender sensibility to feel and resent the lack of accomplishment resulting from the round of conferences, trips, project writing, and budget making, from the busywork of supervising assistants, and from the replication of one set of ideas into a dozen speeches and papers destined to wind up in as many unread proceedings.

The upshot is yet another paradox: turning the theorists into practitioners has made them realize how rare and difficult action is in a crowded world. They pretend to think that the endless exchange of ideas is a universal gain. Actually, they feel less effective than when they used to believe in scholarship *an-und-für-sich*. Some of them, perhaps, would like to change the name of their magazine *Daedalus* to *Sisyphus*.

Third, this private discomfiture is matched by a public one. Judging from what is being studied, researched, fact-found, all over the world, it is clear that as a civilization we no longer know how to do anything simply and directly. We can meet no situation, pursue no purpose, without stopping work and making a study. Nor can we start up again without a period of exploration and testing. We are persuaded that nothing can be done today as it once was done. So we repeatedly analyze the familiar and suspend action. In the end we are as helpless in the face of common need as we are in the face of emergencies. We sit and wait for the reports to tell us what to do, and our self-consciousness grows faster than our knowledge and our will. Only our faith in progress, our faith in the automatism of our methods and our gadgets, keeps us in countenance.

The paradox here is that turning the academic experts loose on the so-called problems of society tends toward this general paralysis. The mania for analyzing and investigating is one form of the well-recognized disorder known in psychiatry by the French name of *folie du doute*. The cure for the disease is obviously a philosophic review of means and ends. But the attempt would require detachment, a proper measure of idleness, and a liberal, as against a professional, outlook. And as we saw, these are the very attributes excluded by the modern design and headlong march of the university.

The liberal outlook is no hidden secret; it is the outlook of the man who is free, because he does not toil for his living, because his responsibilities are of his own choice, and because he can waste time in the pursuit of objects that only he values and understands. Few institutions have come near this kind of freedom. The old, inefficient, absent-minded, bumbling university of the nineteenth century and early twentieth occasionally approached these specifications, and it may still be argued that the products and by-products were not worth the expense. But is our turning it upside down and endways-to any better? All we can say now is that the best part of that tradition looks like a possible antidote to our acute self-poisoning by a deadly mixture of practicality and idealism. At the moment—and I mean at the moment, not necessarily forever—we are, in the apt words of Artemus Ward's *History of England,* "damned by faith, and damned by good works."

12

Scholarship at Gunpoint

The aura of sacredness that surrounds research in the world of business and government comes originally from the graduate school; it is scholarship that first claimed the honor of it and invented the familiar emblems of honest work—footnotes, citations, cross-references, bibliography. Workaday research has a practical use and can also be a frivolous pastime, as will be shown on a later page. And the root idea can turn into caricature, as it has in the lower schools. Anywhere, the emblems can adorn a vacuum of thought, just as statistics can cover up fraud and falsehood. Given these possibilities, what is to be said about research in its original home today?

If one judges by bulk, it is flourishing. Everybody in the academy is at it hand over fist. Looked at closer, the product is seen to be denatured, in two ways: most of it is not re*search* but *re*-search, and the substance is artificially blown up—inflation has set in.

Both defects have come from distorted ideas, of scholarship itself and of what a college and university ought to be. During the past half century, the difference between the two levels of higher education—college and graduate school—has been blurred as regards the role of the professoriate. It is now assumed that the faculty in either place must be composed exclusively of Ph.D's and that these certified scholars will continue to "do research" and publish it. The good repute of the institution demands that they "contribute."

This result was predictable; in fact it was predicted almost

163

as soon as the Ph.D. was invented. William James, Woodrow Wilson, Lawrence Lowell inveighed against its imposition as a prerequisite—as a union card—for college teachers. They knew that not every good learner and teacher has the gift of the true scholar, and they foresaw that the compulsion to act like one would only lead to make-believe scholarship; that is, digging around in published matter for facts and ideas to reproduce in altered words, decorated with the usual emblems. The well-named "scholarly apparatus" guarantees only a mechanical product.

The obvious way out is still open: since the Ph.D. is a fetish, award it after the completion of a master's essay and the passing of the present Ph.D. orals. Not a particle of difference will result in the quality of mind of the degree holder. He or she will have had practice in research by preparing the essay and will possess the same amount of teachable knowledge.

But then the other great mistake of "publish or perish" will have to be reversed. The newly made Ph.D. must no longer be forced to "produce" soon and abundantly so as to "get on the tenure track." The present intolerable (and immoral) pressure on the young teacher has "produced" only an appalling amount of pointless papers—junk research, to go with junk mail and junk bonds: things multiplied without heed to quality.

The side effects upon higher education are many and dire. The worst is the neglect of teaching—there is no time for both research and class preparation. This dilemma is also an obstacle to *scholarly teaching;* for it is clear that working on a little paper means a little subject, whereas the young teacher ought to be keeping up with the scholarship of the broad subject that he teaches. The blight comes from the refusal to admit that a teacher can in fact serve the ideal of scholarship without pushing his findings into print.

What happens now is that a scrap of new information—not knowledge—is presented inside a rehash of the well-known to form a 10-page paper. That operation, repeated without end, accounts for the plethora of journals and books that crowd the library shelves at great expense. What else could be expected? How is it possible to *require* the discovery of truth? As well demand that the prospector *must* strike oil and the major in music compose a masterpiece. If anyone thinks the comparison out of joint, it means that he or she considers scholarship a mediocre pursuit, as indeed it has become.

It is mediocre in language, in thought, and in aim—the last, obviously, since it is for advancement, not discovery. The language is usually jargon, for specialism in imitation of science has made the non-sciences develop terminologies that permit the writer to sound deep when he is only wordy. There may even be an idea in the verbiage, but its value is lost in affectation, which in turn suggests that research is not for the public increase of knowledge; it is an intramural game played for "points" that earn coterie repute and raise in salary.

The game illustrates the difference between specialism and specialization. The latter is inevitable because pre-existing knowledge is extensive. The former takes advantage of this fact to make the most of the least effort by creating subspecialties that few beyond the deviser can enter or understand.

As for the element of thought in research, it is vitiated by each of these practices: specialism leads manifestly to dead-end learning; "publish and perish" compels the young to turn out articles quickly, prolifically, and therefore thoughtlessly—green research, not ripe. Good work takes time, not alone for reflection but also for non-purposive reading. To go to the library and work up a topic in cold blood does not yield lasting scholarship; it lacks the awareness of where the portion of novelty fits into the larger field. As for great work, it is always written out of knowledge that goes miles beyond the subject on all sides.

Equally damaging is the influence of fashion. Modern attitudes are obsessively psychological—finding out the hidden motive, the secret of the mechanism. All the liberal arts have become the playground for research conducted in this spirit. Whether it is the listing of themes and metaphors, or the imputing of unconscious drives or class prejudices, the modern researcher is busy applying a system derived from Fraser or Freud or Marx or some other ideologue in order to proffer startling explanations. In this attempt, thinking in the constructive sense is hardly necessary. One simply lays down a stencil over the well-known material and notes what comes through. An enormous amount of published research is mere enumeration: "Images of Death in the Later Novels of Dickens;" the surrounding comments need be no more than current thought-clichés. The addition to knowledge is not zero, it is a negative quantity, subtracting interest from what was once whole and clear.

More recent schemes of analysis are based on a different failure of thought: making absolute a well-known but relative truth. For example, it is obvious that words have variable meanings; the reality they point to varies with their use and their user. From this observation, some French critics have concluded that no agreement is possible on what words mean; words do not, all things considered, refer to things in reality; indeed, there is no reality; we make it up ourselves. Therefore the works of Shakespeare, the social ideas of Tolstoy, the psychology of Freud are "all fictions we carry in our heads."

By this false inference, the usual diversity of opinion is made to prove that the world consists of minds disconnected from their environment and from each other. This is the error known as the "converse fallacy of accident"—taking a special circumstance to be a general condition.

The fallacy recurs in another destructive form when the ultimate test of scholarship—impartial judgment—is declared illusory. The argument runs: nobody can rid himself entirely of bias; therefore all scholarship is completely biased; therefore let us freely produce propaganda for our views. The refusal to see—or to admit—the difference between a true scholar and a careless or prejudiced one shows lack of candor or inability to think straight—let the partisan choose his category.

The vogue of these two nihilist doctrines strongly suggests that some academic departments have given up serious belief in research; it is but a ritual. Yet seeing through the French critical theory, for one, would be simple enough. When the distinguished foreigner gets a letter inviting him to lecture for a handsome fee, he turns up at the proper time and place because he has relied on the words' reference to reality. And should his check be withheld on the ground that the official letter was only his fiction, he would sue on the basis of the words' clear meaning.

Similarly, though opinions differ about literature, *Hamlet* is not about the Trojan War, nor *The Iliad* about a boy running away from home on the Mississippi River. Starting from these demonstrable facts, scholarship used to point out other, less visible, but widely recognizable meanings by exact reference to the text. But now "there is no text." A speaker at a professional conference was asked whether the new dogma would still allow a scholar to tell a student he was misinterpreting a particular passage. "Certainly not! That would be unforgivable arrogance." If so, scholarly criticism is no longer possible and the enterprise—the academic departments—should shut up shop.

In another kind of research, the kind labeled educational, the same futility obtains, for different reasons. It patterns itself on psychology and relies on statistics, without realizing how inapplicable the results are to what goes on in the classroom. Except for Piaget's direct observation of very young children, educational research is content to use tests, add up scores, and make up jargon for doubtful suppositions. Even supposing that the tests are well made, what they are believed to be testing are abstractions—intelligence, mathematical ability, self-esteem. These do not exist as *things,* they are not made up of units to be counted; they are constructs to begin with, which then are inferred from answers to miscellaneous questions. The research is at two removes from life.

Nor is this all. Statistical significance, which is what the "study" reports, does not mean significance in the ordinary sense of importance. It is only a measure of probability that tells nothing about good results or preferable means. Nor is correlation a sign of causation, as so many studies assume. The research there stands at three removes from classroom reality. When according to one famous report, the quality of a school is said to have nothing to do with how well the students learn, it is time to turn to other authorities.

These others may be known by their language; they write intelligibly. They are observers; their facts are derived from seeing what goes on and making judgments based on reasons rather than scores. If numbers are used they are of persons and things, not abstract entities. To keep abreast of our present troubles, read such experts as Lynne Cheney, Diane Ravitch, Arn Tibbetts, Donald Cowan, Edward G. Efros, John Illo, Gerald D. Bracey, Chester Finn, James P. Degnan, and the late Lawrence Cremin.

Educational researchers have lately said they were "vexed," because their work is not being heeded in the present emergency. Thinking back to the workings of look-and-say and other schemes adopted after research, one is not disposed to support the complaint. And it would be absurd to suppose much of value lurks in the innumerable "findings" that were fortunately not acted on and subsidized. It is clear that in this kind of research also the pressure to publish has multiplied the output. Mass production, which can make material goods abundant and serviceable, does not repeat the miracle for products of the mind: it only makes them abundant.

"Doing Research"—Should the Sport Be Regulated?

. . . .

Washington, D.C. Alumni Club, December 16, 1986;
Columbia Magazine, February 1987

Listen to conversations, inside the academy or outside, and you discover that "doing research" is the true vocation of modern man. Next to being Picasso or conducting the Philharmonic, research is the one activity that is self-justifying. This attitude is remarkable in many ways, for the name research applies to widely different purposes that vary in kind and importance. There is laboratory research in science or medicine. There is industrial research. And there is market research, which is not conducted in a laboratory but maybe in the street, ringing doorbells and asking searching questions about the best name for a new detergent. People employed by magazines to verify dates and middle initials are called researchers because they know how to use the dictionary and the *Columbia Encyclopedia.*

But these familiar occupations do not exhaust the list. Any well-trained college graduate can find a job as a researcher in a bank, in business, in a private foundation, in a charity, in a lobby or political action group, in a government bureau. Every day the mail brings unsolicited "studies" from such places. They may be honest or tendentious, but they are all born of some species of research showing its earmarks of tables and graphs and footnotes and bibliography. Seeing all this, one may say that the virus of scholarship, the academic bug, has been endlessly contagious. It has escaped through the campus gates and brought on conditions of mind and work that are now universal.

Because these have developed gradually and for what seemed useful ends, we do not notice how new they are in the world. For example, we tend to take libraries for granted, as if they had always existed in their present guise. We should remember that such things as library science and the uniform catalogue card, the possibility of public access to all collections, the faith that anything can be *looked up* if only one knows where to go— all this is 20th-century innovation.

Being specialists, we also need to be reminded that the total number of published lists, repertories, manuals, guides, digests, books of facts, and single-subject encyclopedias is enormous. With the computer at hand, entire publishing concerns have arisen to put together or reprint these shortcuts to research. You can look up in a single book the names and biographies of animals in fiction and you can find a comparable roster of all the governors of the United States since 1789. Besides which, there are lists of lists, reference books about reference books.

As for journals, they proliferate like rabbits as specialties divide like amoebas—or as contributors grow impatient with slow-publishing quarterlies and start a new organ so that their red-hot papers may not cool. Take a rather diffident academic subject: philosophy. There are 71 journals for a group of readers all over the world which, if divided evenly, would provide each journal with a subscription list of under 300. We write faster than we read, and the steady stream of half-price sale catalogues from university presses shows that the production of scholarly books for rare readers is as copious as that of journals.

I have been citing academic research. Multiply what I have described by the number of other fields and interests, and you begin to get a sense of the tremendous volume of ostensible facts being both poured out over us and put into bottles for others. This vast system supports our insatiable desire to find out and record and "make available." It is admirable and impressive, but it has a reverse side, which comes into view when we ask: How good is this output and what is it good for?

In the workaday world it is clear that most of what is proffered as research is secondhand and dubious. The magazine researchers find *one* reference and think a fact or judgment confirmed. Opinion research is continually shown up by its results. Gallup gives one figure, Harris another. And in the stream of reports about divorce, disease, and diet, about education, ecology, economics, and government, indeed about all subjects of practical concern, the chaos is permanent and daunting. One could write a novel of adventure with Cholesterol as the hero, now pictured as the villain, now innocent unless provoked.

It is safe to say that the steady stream of "studies" does not really add to the public's knowledge. One report cancels another; details do not stick in the mind; and interest is too often aroused by what goes against common sense. Thus the National Institute on Aging has found that having sympathetic friends and relatives at times of grief may be harmful. Solitary widows fare as well or better. Should the world, enlightened on this point, considerately neglect the afflicted? What is certain is that findings may harm the many who interpret them as absolute and universal. The researchers who studied the chances of marriage for women who postponed it in a good cause heard cries of anger and despair as if they had passed a law on the subject. All these studies rely on correlations, and some on the fallacy of *post hoc ergo propter hoc*.

Moreover, it is obvious that the citizen at large does not read the actual research report; he or she has only the newspaper or magazine story. So, in answering the questions how good and how useful is the research offered daily to the public, one must say that it is largely without influence and sometimes damaging. The net effect is to load the mind with halfhearted superstitions: "I've read somewhere that sneezing too much is a sign of heart disease." The remark came from a highly intelligent person. Imagine what the heads of the uncritical must be stuffed with. The genuine knowledge in publicized research does not get lodged in the public mind. It stay inside the profession, to be fought over by rival theorists.

That fact brings us back to academic research; for not only does the form of the studies we read about follow the canons of academic scholarship, but many of its producers are also members of a university. Looking at universities tells us why and how the great Niagara of research flows over our heads.

The original source takes its rise at the beginning of this century in what William James called "the Ph.D. Octopus," which dictates that every member of the academic force can and should be a productive scholar—a novel idea in the history of scholarship. It used to be the other way around. The stereotype of the scholar was that of an old bookworm who amassed learning year after year without ever getting to his great book. To suppose that every owner of a Ph.D. can carry on valuable research while also teaching and find time to write it up in publishable form, is contrary to fact; motive and ability are not to be had on demand. The true scholar might devote a lifetime to a large subject and publish on the brink of the grave. Now, after the dissertation's painful birth, the scholar must give signs of fertility every couple of years.

All sorts of bad things follow: the articles that help justify the young professor's existence can only deal with small points, a matter of detail or interpretation of detail. So the footnote that it deserves is blown up into an article. By the same method what should be an article becomes a book.

This practice has curious side effects. The research done to discover and launch the small squib means reading the latest periodical literature, which is made up of the same sort of bloated matter. Older, more solid books are considered out-of-date and are no longer relied on. The result is that quite often the new fact turns out to be already on record, anticipated by a worker of the 1880s or 90s, who set it down in its proper place—a footnote in a large work.

A worse by-product of modern inflation is that it defeats the very purpose of compulsory scholarship: that purpose was to engineer the growth of knowledge by having as many trained workers as possible add their little brick to the edifice. The outcome in fact is that the torrent of books and papers steadily increases the unlikelihood of any synthesis. Plowing through the mass of reports lengthens the task while it confuses the mind. Minutiae come to look important because they occupy space.

Of course, as soon as one begins to talk about synthesis and large, important subjects requiring years of study, one is met by an objection which is also an excuse. "There is so much to know that the field must be split up. You can do your job thoroughly only if you narrow your purview. I'll work in one little corner without going into yours—so kindly leave mine alone."

One may question whether the product of this specialism *is* knowledge. A moment ago, I raised a doubt whether the mass of research on practical matters helped the public. But surely in intellectual matters, there can be no doubt: knowledge does not exist for society unless widely known, and felt, and used. What specialism gives us is at best information. We speak of computers as data banks; we ought to speak of learned journals as safe-deposit boxes, double-locked against outsiders. This is why the so-called knowledge explosion, at least in the humanities and historical sciences, is mainly an explosion of the library stacks.

Mention of the library turns our mind back to the source books, manuals, bibliographies, and the like that I cited as evidence of the cult of research. By worshipping at the shrine of fact, we seem to have worked ourselves into a vicious circle. We turn out articles and reports in profusion; somebody has to abstract the ever-growing bulk into reference books for the research community. But we do not put the original articles through the shredding machine. We keep them to make more articles possible. We keep everything. Think of the "presidential papers" in the presidential houses that pop up in state after state. In New York, Governor Carey wanted and obtained $10 million to publish his deathless words in their natural setting of memos and telex. Other governors are sure to hear of this glorification, and it will not be long before a sense of fair play makes us give equal space to lieutenant governors—for the sake of future researchers.

Only one group, it seems, has exercised restraint: the professors of law. Just a couple of months ago, their association complained that its members did not contribute enough to the jamboree of research. Much is said these days against lawyers, but this abstinence should be chalked up to their credit. These teachers of law attend to their business of teaching, and those that publish—for there are some—apparently do so when they have something to say.

The predicament of unmanageable excess is new, but it was foreseen 40 years ago. At Columbia, Robert Lynd, the co-author of the famous *Middletown,* asked in a thoughtful essay "Knowledge for What?" At the University of Chicago, the Italian historian Gaetano Salvemini said we must give up what he called the encyclopedic ideal of research—making sure to see everything before writing a line. The novelist E. M. Forster, who was classically trained, insisted that modern scholarship was only pseudo-scholarship; unlike the classical kind, it cannot survey all the available evidence. *Pseudo* is too harsh a word, suggesting pretense if not fakery. But the paradox is true that the more we research and pile up data, the less is thoroughness attainable. Therefore uncertainty grows in proportion to the fruitfulness of research.

In this deluge of factuality, the cultural pressure of science is manifest. Everybody naturally wants his or her views to be accepted and believed, and in our culture the way to achieve this is to make the message look like science. This reflection raises the question whether the natural scientists themselves are happy about the state of their research. Those I have talked with over the years—some physicists and biologists, a good many psychologists and medical doctors—are *not* happy. They say that most published papers are routine performances, pointless and often repetitive. And since space in scientific journals is scarce, these papers are presumably choice productions from among a much larger output of triviality.

I give this judgment at second hand and in passing, so as to lay the ground for a suggestion later on, and also to bring up one more aspect of research closer to my own work. I refer to *quantification* in the humanities and social sciences. Another term often used for it is *measurement,* but that is a misnomer. In these subjects quantifying is only counting. Measurement implies a homogeneous substance that can be divided into equal parts by means of a standard unit devised for the purpose. In quantified research, the homogeneous substance is seldom more than a verbal abstraction. When, for example, "violence" preceding a revolution is quantified, or the "education" of the Tudor nobility, or "religion" in our own time, the material is not there to be handled; it is only assumed to be a uniform substance, which is then pseudo-measured by means of "indicators." Violence is quantified from police reports, Tudor education from matriculation at Oxford and Cambridge, current religion from church attendance. But these indicators are wobbly: one can attend church and not be religious. In scholarship about the arts similar practices are in vogue. In music, for example, certain formulas and devices are given the role of indicators in order to arrive at a numerical idea of a composer's "style." Why this needs to be done is hard to explain. Style can be ascertained better and more cheaply at a good performance.

In sociology, in music, in every subject of interest, it is the computer that has encouraged this sort of research. To feed its hunger, researchers have opened up unused collections of facts, ranging from police-station dockets to the mistakes of Shakespeare's typesetters. The assumption here is that a large number of small items, insignificant in themselves, can when added up yield important truths. So far nothing of profound importance has emerged. The interesting work, the great work, continues to be done in the traditional way by men and women who have something to say: they are not simply "doing research."

What then, is to be done about this expensive hobby, which, unlike a sport, is unscheduled, has no umpire, and is carried on whether there are spectators or not? Clearly, regulation is out of the question. The first amendment protects equally the wise man and the fool—quite rightly, for some apparent fools turn out to be wise. The only applicable force is that of public opinion. In the natural sciences, where the public is small and trained and bent on making headway, the useless and the absurd are quickly got rid of—by neglect. True, sometimes a good scientific idea is neglected for many years; it happened in geology about tectonics, the movement of continental plates. But on the whole, the rubbish-disposal system is efficient and fair.

It is in other realms of thought that we wallow ever deeper in folly and falsehood or plain ignorance, when we might be well-informed. And those realms are the ones we inhabit from day to day—the subjects that deal with man in society, beginning with history and going on to literature and the arts, philosophy, and the essence of mind itself.

On reflection I see a few possibilities of self-defense. First, put an end to publish or perish. The recent, highly critical Carnegie Report gives a hint that the academic world might recover sanity by a dose of Know-Thyself. It would have the useful consequence of restoring judgment—the judgment of the able by their peers. As things stand now, judgment is by weight in ounces of printed paper.

A second measure, to be taken by the general public, is to rehabilitate common sense. I do not mean by this the rejection offhand of what is new or unfamiliar. I mean the thoughtful conclusions of experience, individual and social. When research declares that the quality of a school is of no effect, it is permissible not merely to doubt but to deny.

This application of common sense is a daily requirement, and journalists ought to be the first to exercise it. When some time ago an American historian published results to the effect that the railroads had not influenced the economic development of the country, there should have ensued a mournful silence, not publicity. Such studies unconsciously ape certain kinds of modern art—startling and contrived. After careful scrutiny they should receive the treatment formerly accorded to naughty boys, for the attention sought is that given to the enfant terrible.

Sometimes, of course, projects conceal their own fatuity by being mysterious. I remember, in the early days of Fulbright fellowships, sitting on a committee that had to pass on a proposal to study "The Influence of Psychic Images on Obesity in Singers."

175

The latter part of the statement sounded as if well-rooted in fact, though the earlier part was cloudy. It took two of us an appreciable time to persuade the others that the psychological fantasy was not worth a Fulbright. To be sure, the use of common sense as defined entails a risk, but there is no remedy without risk, and a desirable side effect would follow. I mean an increased resistance to the rhetoric of fact and the rhetoric of number. We have been so conditioned by genuine science to the mere statement, "these are the facts, these are the numbers," that like Pavlov's dogs we submit without question, often in the teeth of contrary evidence. To modern faith, the figures denote fact, whereas words are opinion—as if opinion were not a fact too, and the figure often a guess. Once more, the Carnegie Report—though it comes 30 years late—is a hopeful sign. It recommends getting rid of SATs.

The best means of rescuing research in the long run is the steady encouragement of solid, manifestly useful undertakings. In the modern infatuation with research, these are at a disadvantage: they look regular, not innovative; they call for sober work, not fancy techniques; they promise utility along recognized lines, not amazing revelations and upside-down revisionism. With common sense in charge, the superstitious regard for "doing research" could be held in check, if not dispelled, and the genuine investigation of great subjects might once more give to research and its products the value and the praise they used to deserve.

13

Campus Martius = Field of the God of War

It can be assumed that many of the college-bound arrive on campus with other things in mind than to drink and take drugs, cheat on exams, and commit gang rapes, though they soon come across opportunities as well as examples of such behavior. But other forms of self-expression that have little to do with education also exist, and these become part of the student's life as spectator or participant, because condoned and often encouraged by the authorities.

To put it briefly, the college or university, no longer a republic, is now a democracy of a peculiar kind. Just as the public school took on the task of reform, so the academy has taken on the role of showcase. Here cultural, political, and ethnic pluralism would prevail. Overt teaching and official policy would show how enlightened men and women think and act in modern society and train their charges to follow the same high principles.

As usual, a laudable purpose pursued with an instrument meant for something else has recoiled and turned what was less than perfect into the positively bad. This worsened state of the campus is familiar to every concerned parent and every reader of the news. A law in Wisconsin requires every college to inform prospective students of its crime rate for the preceding year. But before this battlefield condition became general, guerrilla attitudes had set in. The first casualty was free speech. Whether members of the faculty or guest speakers, persons known or sus-

177

pected of harboring the wrong views on the issues of the day were denied a hearing, often in tumultuous and offensive fashion.

This is the sign of the peculiar democracy. It works by verbal onslaught and physical disruption, the small group coercing the large community into submission. And naturally, assault begets retaliation in an endless round. This is often called the politicizing of higher education. That term is much too good for what has happened. Politics is a normal endeavor, rough or smooth, to obtain a tangible result for a public or private end. What is being witnessed on campuses from Dartmouth to Berkeley is faction and feuding for intangibles and abstractions. What gets satisfied is malice, vanity, revenge, and kindred feelings. The Montagus and Capulets were at least paying each other back for the death of relatives. In the universities today the printed or posted attacks, the vandalism, the protests and counterprotests, the demand for resignations, the sit-ins and strikes are caused partly by academic measures and fees that the students dislike, but more often by group slurs, tasteless jokes, or imputed inequality of treatment—outcroppings of Chauvinism, male and female, black and white, sex type A and sex type B. It is a Balkan campus with border incidents, not party politics.

The very phrase "lack of sensitivity," which is the usual recrimination, shows that it is not political will that is at work, but hair-trigger susceptibility. A professor of law is found to have quoted in his textbook two lines from Byron on the nature of woman. He is excoriated like a scoundrel. Another faculty member publishes in the student paper a letter part of which is misunderstood by some readers. He is treated like a pariah because, after the sense has been re-expounded, he "did not once apologize for the misunderstanding"—others' misreading was his fault.

That last instance, mild as it appears, actually gives the diagnostic trait of the evil: public outcry to make others suffer, even for imaginary or inadvertent wrongs. The practice is not limited to student groups on the watch for offense. Instructors associating themselves with a group may rid the class of a student who asks a civil question, if by interpretation it seems to criticize the group. Frequently, the college administration apologizes on behalf of the alleged offender and orders him or her to submit to special counseling for a stretch of "sensitivity training." It should be: training to remember who is above criticism.

For it is clear that plenty of persons and professions, of nations and ethnic groups, can be humiliated and insulted without blame—to begin with, the speakers who are invited and then booed and yelled out of the hall. Likewise the many minorities as yet unorganized. In New York City, one kind of taxi that is not fully licensed is known as a gypsy cab. Now the Gypsies, an ancient people from Northwest India, have long suffered contumely, and worse. Under Hitler, half a million—one in ten of the entire people—were killed in the gas chambers. Perhaps twice that number live in the United States. They do not like the name that we give them and that we use to disparage dubious things. But until a leader organizes a demonstration that blocks Fifth Avenue and makes *gypsy* a recognized slur, all New Yorkers and other Americans will keep uttering the degrading term; and when in the country during the summer, they will continue to blame the ruin of their trees on the detestable gypsy moth.

The point of this illustration is that a free-for-all type of democracy is never a free-for-*all*. But if in self-defense the whole world organized itself into clans, life would indeed be brutish and short. Only in a state of modest self-restraint, of civil speech and mutual deference can someone who is part of a truly pluralistic body hope to meet with general respect and substantial equality. In such a state every person is regarded first and last as an individual, not a representative of some embattled social group or vested interest.

It was precisely that state which the former university had achieved and destroyed. The break with decency dates from the student uprisings of 1965–68. Instead of articulating their true grievances, which were many and genuine, the students attacked the institution as such, with violence and for reasons outside its purview, such as the draft for the Vietnam war. The bewildered academics responded with shuffling and cowardice, thus failing once more in their duty to teach. The outcome was to turn over the university to the loudest claimants, then and in future. Can it be that the current combativeness, practiced as an end in itself, owes its zest to the graduates of that era now occupying faculty chairs?

Be that as it may, the legacy of '68 is visible in the new order, which relies on written codes and quasi judicial hearings, on make-believe "open competition" for administrative posts, on scrutiny by departments into their recruits' opinions, on suspicion and indignation as the ruling passions, on the pretext of "academic freedom" to exclude from the campus the representatives of certain government agencies and "tainted" business corporations, and on the make-up of the curriculum as a weapon in the race- class- sex-struggle.

But isn't the university in the world and bound to take part in its battles—in fact, to lead its most aggressive efforts toward justice and equality? *Bound* begs the question and does not answer *how?* One might as well ask, Isn't the doctor in the same room with the patient and bound to suffer with him? Well, sympathy he must certainly have as part of his healing power, but he must precisely not hamper himself by internalizing the symptoms and the pain. He must stand off and study the case. And that is what the universities were supposed to do.

. . . Supposed to do *at the university.* Its members are free like other citizens to engage on their own time in any social and political struggle they choose. They live in townships and counties organized for the rough-and-tumble of a real democracy, which a university is not. That is why its proper work stops when a quite lawless democracy enters in. A university is not a town, even though it assembles 25,000 people on its acreage. It cannot be decently run by campaigning and voting on "issues." What rival platforms can express the "interests" of the College as against those of the School of Dentistry? Or those of any two "parties" within each?

Even if this were possible, the shouting and accusing and tampering with the truth that are the stuff of politics are the rank opposite of the academic principle. There is hidden virtue in the dismissive phrase: "purely academic." Its proper meaning is that thought should precede action, that is to say, theory devised freely and refined by argument before being applied. The saving in cost and trouble is plain. Social and scientific advance comes from the purely academic when it has been much revised and finally confirmed in practice. But the academy is not its testing ground. When it tries to be, it forgets its own role—as we see it doing—and neglects its unique duty.

What is most dispiriting about colleges and universities today is that they have regressed to earlier defects. For a long time the American college was a place for young bloods to be rowdies. In the age of Jefferson's University of Virginia, faculty members (and their wives) could expect molestation and violence; student hostility toward teachers was *de rigueur.* (A milder strain of it comes out today in the "evaluation" blanks that make teaching a popularity contest and thus encourage low standards of work: a good grade for a good evaluation.)

The gentlemanly tradition of college violence lasted well into the 19th century. But by the end of the Civil War, it was something else that plagued the faculty. Big universities were set up to raise the quality of scholarship and professional training to the level attained abroad; private donors gave huge sums and state legislatures adopted handsome budgets. One result was that trustees and lawmakers monitored opinion: radical thought, cultural dissent was not tolerated. Tocqueville's old dictum that he knew of "no country with so little independence of thought and freedom of expression as the United States" was repeatedly verified.

But there was resistance to censorship and persecution. The test of strength came in the 1920s. When President Lowell of Harvard told the Overseers, who wanted him to dismiss the Socialist lecturer Harold Laski, "If you demand his resignation you will have mine tomorrow," the right to impart scholarly opinion was finally won. Lowell defined it in a classic paragraph which protected equally those with and without tenure. It was not contested even in the years of Marxist propaganda during the Great Depression. The honor of the American university shone bright for not quite half a century.

If one looks back to a period still earlier than American beginnings, that is, to the first universities of the late Middle Ages, one readily sees that the special function of a university does not survive the pseudo democracy of shifting control by warring groups. The end comes with a bang and suppression follows—or reconstitution on saner lines. That being so, one can only hope that life on the campus today will get rapidly worse, so that shame and despair may awaken recollections of a decent past, after which dedicated spirits will strive to reestablish the due forms and civil temper of a company of scholars.

Back to the Middle Ages

Saturday Review, November 15, 1969;
In Defense of Academic Freedom, ed. Sidney Hook, Pegasus,
New York, 1971; *Nichibei Forum* (in Japanese) June 1970; and
ten other re-printings in the U.S., Canada, Sweden,
and the Philippines

There are not sixteen ways of running a college or university. Except for interesting but inessential variations, there are only three, and not all three yield to the same extent the conditions favorable to study.

Let us look at the earliest—student power. It marked the very beginnings of universities. The typical precedents are Bologna and Paris; Bologna shows the internal relationships; Paris the day-to-day workings. In both universities the idea was participation. Authority lay with the general assembly. There was no distinct central organization, but a loose collection of units. The *universitas* or corporation was the name of this grouping, which implied nothing academic.

At Bologna, the students soon seized control, thereby expressing the burghers' control of the city. The sons dictated to the professors, and the city fathers backed up the youthful will by law. For example, professors and doctors could not leave the university, under penalty of death, or even go out of town without permission. They had to swear absolute obedience to the student-elected student rector, who at the behest of the general assembly could pass or change any rule. The students collected the fees, paid the salaries, and issued the working rules. If the teacher cut a class, he was fined; likewise, if he could not draw five students, if he skipped a chapter or a difficulty, or if he kept on talking after the ringing of the bell. At any time the lecturer could be interrupted by a beadle summoning him to appear before the rector and learn of his misdeeds.

As the great historian of universities, Rashdall, puts it—and notice in passing that boycott is the true name for student strike or sit-in: "By means of the terrible power of boycotting which they could bring into play against any offending professor, the student clubs were masters of the situation." Not until Bonaparte conquered Italy five centuries later was a professor again considered fit to be rector of a university.

Rashdall's reference to student clubs brings us to the situation at Paris. Medieval students were divided into "nations," just as the teachers were divided into subject-matter faculties. But the nation soon ceased to denote birthplace and became an arbitrary aggregate. The French nation at Paris included Spaniards, Italians, Greeks, and Levantines; the English took in Flemings, Scandinavians, Finns, Hungarians, Dutch, and Slavs—no British insularity then! These clubs were further divided into clans usually based on parish allegiance. Here was no compact group of bourgeois fathers' sons, but an international and vagrant crowd of large proportions. The results for university governance were to be expected—incessant quarrels, shaky alliances, jealous betrayals.

For each nation had to vote as one unit in the assembly and elect a new rector *each month*. They voted on proctors, beadles, financial officers, examiners, and deans. They also had to choose one ad hoc committee after another to look into endless charges and abuses. In the great year 1266, the papal legate Simon de Brie tried in vain to get the rector's term extended to six weeks, in hopes of reducing the number of contested elections and student defiance of the rectors and the rules. At one time two rectors claimed authority. Simon finally got them both to resign in exchange for a statute permitting a nation to secede and thus escape disputed rules. This feud of 1266 lasted a good fifteen years.

The suggestive point in this truly flexible system is that it went on all fours with the prevailing theory of government—

"what affects all must be by the consent of all." It was democracy to the full. A representative body was not supposed to express the collective will of its constituents but to give every individual will a chance. Three students (out of several thousand) could ask for a change of statutes, and officers were elected who specialized in statute-changing.

The frequent elections fitted in with the reigning philosophy. Aristotle had said that no one should be entrusted with any but the briefest tenure of office and that the whole assembly must not only legislate but administer. And student control obviously meant a deal of administering—collecting fees, paying salaries, renting or buying school buildings, watching the financial officers, approving student lodgings, supervising book publishers (copyists), issuing summonses, levying fines, and seeing to the taking of oaths on an unprecedented scale.

All this plus the fights of town and gown and the internal feuds that, according to one authority, were "akin to later international wars in their ferocity and destructiveness," must have made the student life rich and exciting. Everything was an issue, including the hiring of messengers, of which the several nations had from twelve to 160 each. A touching detail of organization was that the rector might bring to the meetings of the assembly his bosom friend as a bodyguard.

This elaborate structure so far was all for administration. Not a word yet about the *studium,* the classwork. The rector, students, and (elected) deans looked after it very much as was done at Bologna, that is, by supervising the professors. This arrangement called for certain abilities in the rector, and since the freshmen, who were eligible, often were under the entrance age of fourteen, the Paris rules came to stipulate that the rector must be at least twenty years old.

One can imagine these eager, free-lance, turn-and-turn-about administrators as belonging to the group of older students and apprentice teachers, the bold and daring, handsome and articulate—those who, like M. Cohn-Bendit in our day, glory in the feeling of "we do what we like."

One can, again, imagine them angry at the previous administration, impatient with the snarls of bureaucracy that they could so quickly fix by some further rules, exhilarated at the thought of the coming meeting with a good fight in prospect, and ready always for the actual bloodshed on the narrow winding street, if townsmen or a gang from the wrong parish or nation should debouch from the next corner.

As one describes the scene, one is suddenly hushed at the thought of François Villon gathering up his genius amid the confusion and surviving as the symbol of an emancipated day. Was he perhaps one of those excluded as "vagabond scholars" from taking part in the making of the curriculum, the degree requirements, the class schedules and examinations, and the plan of festivities? Or was he one of the many non-scholars, those hangers-on mysteriously called "martinets"? No one knows, but some of his brilliance and energy must have existed elsewhere in the mass, or there would have been no medieval university, no medieval mind to write about.

University administration by student groups is not to be sneezed at. It is cheap and never monotonous. By controlling the faculty it certainly prevents the flight from teaching, and it affords the young the pleasure of making their elders hop, skip, and perform. In fighting all of society and themselves, too, the medieval students preserved minority rights to a degree otherwise unexampled. That is, such rights were freely enjoyed by the victors and survivors of the scrimmage. The rest—well, there is a price to pay for every good thing, and the good achieved was the very appealing, youthful kind of life: the free-for-all.

Besides, student power need not be as perpetually violent as it was in the glorious thirteenth century. It can be had at the somewhat lower price of a lack of continuity and a repetition of hopeful errors; for in one student generation experience hardly has a chance to accumulate and make a difference; and who cares in youth about the confusion that comes of injecting practical and political action into the rather different atmosphere of study?

The second mode of managing universities is illustrated by what happened when the confusion became too great—or at least when it seemed to the neighbors to have got out of hand. An historian of the time who, as legal representative of the university, cannot have been prejudiced against it says: "Studies were in chaos . . .

185

the rooms on one side were rented to students and the others to whores. Under the same roof was a house of learning and of whoring." There was no reason in the nature of youth itself why this boisterous exercise of self-government and self-indulgence should stop. But by 1500 the scheme was swept away in the collapse of the medieval theory and practice of government. In one short generation—by 1530—a new University of Paris was in being.

The force at work was the rise of the nation state, the movement that gave "nation" its modern meaning. The One Hundred Years' War had shown the country's need for an effective central power to put down disorders and stop the waste. That power was the king, and it was the king who put an end to student power within the university. In 1450, he restrained their excessive feasting. He then ordered the papal legate to reform the university from top to bottom. By 1475 he was imposing a loyalty oath and, soon after, threatening students with a kind of draft. Finally, in 1499, he prohibited their boycotts and battles.

From then on, whether under king or revolutionary government, dictator or Parliament, continental universities have been ruled by the central authority. The degree of control has varied widely with time and place. Still, out of ancestral respect for learning, the European university has always enjoyed certain privileges. For example, even under the Russian czars the police were forbidden to enter the university, a tradition that curiously persisted through the Russian repression of Czechoslovakia in the summer of 1968.

No one needs to be told that in times of trouble since 1500, universities under central control have been threatened, dictated to, or shut down; professors suspended for sedition, exiled for refusing to take oaths, prosecuted and shot for political crimes, and, from the beginning to the twentieth century, periodically heckled, insulted, or physically attacked by their own students. These appear to be inevitable by-products of making the university political through its link with the state.

Central control is, of course, the opposite of student power, but they have one feature in common—the multiplicity of rules. When codes and tribunals regulate university affairs, the legalistic outlook and the contentious temper prevail and warp the emotions appropriate to study. And contrary to expectations, even the man-agement of the university's material concerns is not thereby im-proved but worsened. The reason is plain. Both these styles of administration—the anarchical and the autocratic—bring to the fore people whose temperaments are the reverse of studious and scholarly.

Imagine the American university going down the road it has lately chosen and becoming thoroughly reactionary, which is to say, going back to either of these earlier modes of governance. In the one case, that of student power, we should see the emergence of a new type of academic man, wanting and achieving power at a much younger age than his predecessors—in fact, a graduate student or beginning teacher. He would be a man of strong feel-ings, caught by some sort of doctrine, ready to drop his work at any time for the turbulence of mass meetings and the stress of political tactics, and not averse to exchanging blows when denun-ciation, blackmail, and obscenity fail—a man, in short, prepared to strike in all senses of the word; a man given to the life of im-pulse and self-will, like the old-fashioned duelist, and also given to the heady pleasure of moral indignation; a man ever suspi-cious—and with good reason; a partisan, but restless, dissatisfied with all arrangements including his own, because his idealism and his strength alike drive him to find a life totally free of *conditions*.

We need not ask whether men such as this in a reactionary university would wield their power in behalf of an outside politi-cal party, as in the Japanese university, and use professors as in-dentured servants closely supervised. The texture of the strait-jacket might be looser, owing to the presence of diverse student leaders similarly moved to have their way.

But we cannot doubt that an opposite reaction to central control would bring with it the enforcement of a political ortho-doxy. The type of man who would rise in such a system is quickly described: the commissar with a Ph.D. And he too would be a poor provider of the complex physical arrangements prerequisite to study: His mind would be incessantly on things so much higher. He would have no doctrine but order, and after a few faculty-club shootings, seminars would meet on time.

The third mode of university administration is the one we

have so rashly abandoned over the space of a few months. The American university was a characteristic creation. Drawing on the old English collegiate model for its best habits, it assumed that the faculty *was* the university, and as such the protector of two great treasures—students and learning. Learning was something to be transmitted to the young and added to when possible. Study was thus the single aim for both faculty and students.

The running of academic affairs by a faculty through a mixture of convention and consensus was, of course, easier when the faculty was small and its members lived close together. But the triumph of the American universities is that between 1890 and 1950 many of them grew to the size of a town yet kept the spirit and action of the original free university, the university governed not by the one or the many, but by principles.

These principles were simple enough: influence and deference; rationality and civility; above all, reciprocity.

Most people, including some academic men, had, of course, no idea how American or any other universities were run and could discern no principles whatever in the day-to-day operations. So when the cry of tyranny and revolt was raised, they rushed to pull down the fabric, on the assumption that where there's a complaint there must be an evil. The questions of what evil and where it lay precisely were never thought of. Indignation in some, passivity in others conspired to establish as a universal truth that the American university was an engine of oppression, rotten to the core, a stinking anachronism. So down it came.

That it must stay down for a good while appears inevitable from the nature of its former freedom. How was it free? Not because its members were angels and its statutes copied from Utopia, but because its concentration on study had brought the world at large to respect its autonomy—hence, no interference from the state—while freedom of thought and speech had generated within the walls the principles listed above. The free university is that in which the scholar and teacher is free to learn and to teach. He is free because society values and keeps its hands off the double product—the learning student on one side, new knowledge on the other.

Principles, of course, need devices for their application and protection. The American university had evolved some fairly good ones for the purpose: 1) The trustees (or regents or legislative committees), whose defined role showed that they did not own the university, nor were employers of employees; they bestowed tenure as a guaranty against themselves.

2) The administration, conceived again not as bosses but as servants; easily removed if unsatisfactory; in practice, a body that worked like slaves to suit faculty wishes and that protected scholars against trustees as well as against parents and alumni.

3) The professional associations—learned, accrediting, or self-serving like the American Association of University Professors—all upholders of academic freedom.

4) Public opinion, the law, and the press, which until very recent years could be counted on to keep hands off and even defend the individual scholar, researcher, discoverer, expert.

At each level, the attitude of the imperfect beings entrusted with administrative responsibilities was that they could only influence the action of others, not command it; that decisions must be rational and discussions civil; that any signs of strong reluctance after discussion must be deferred to, and that rights and duties, like concessions, must be reciprocal.

This is not to say that the institution always worked like a dream. Friction, abuses, injustice beset all human undertakings. But no one can deny that compared with other institutions, universities enjoyed a government in keeping with their high purpose—government by separation of powers, by consent through committees, and by extensive self-restraint. Within the best universities and colleges there was continuous consultation, a wide tolerance of eccentricity and free-wheeling, a maximum of exceptions and special attention—and these latitudes had long since been extended to the students.

In recalling this fast-waning institution, one may indeed think of occasions when the principles were violated. But one should also think of the great diversity of opinion and of purpose that was permitted to flourish, even when challenged. For example: boards of trustees, generally Republican and conservative, allowing leaves to professors working in Washington for the New Deal or for John Kennedy; or in the Thirties ignoring the Communist affiliation even of junior officers without tenure. Go back fifty years and you will think of the protectors of Veblen and his work, of defiant instruction in Marxism, of research and indoctrination in contraception.

Nor should we forget the common realities of the last half century—the open campus, receptive to all the shocking modern literature and subversive speakers; the college newspapers receiving subsidies from administrators they denounce and insult by name; the frequent public championing of dissent, as when President Brewster of Yale stood between angry alumni and Professor Staughton Lynd.

Fifteen years ago, Walter P. Metzger, the leading authority on academic freedom, summed up the extraordinary character of the American university: "No one can follow the history of academic freedom without wondering at the fact that any society, interested in the immediate goals of solidarity and self-preservation, should possess the vision to subsidize free criticism and inquiry, and without feeling that the academic freedom we still possess is one of the remarkable achievements of man. At the same time, one cannot but be appalled at the slender thread by which it hangs."

When certain students, with encouragement from many sides, cut the thread, they did it (as they thought) in the name of still greater freedom. They wanted a "voice," and, with a trifle of self-contradiction, a "dialogue" on "non-negotiable demands." Sentimentalists believed that the university "bulldozed the student," carried on "a war against the young." The truth is that for years student opinion had been exerting an influence on curriculum and campus rules and habits, not only through free expression in the sacrosanct student paper, but, more importantly, through free access to faculty members and ease of deportment with them. Go to Europe and Asia and see how they "interact" there.

The common faith in education as an individual right had also made the student's free choice among programs and courses the accepted thing, while the combining of programs, the multiplicity of certificates and degrees, the preservation of credits through all changes of mind—all these practices encouraged even to excess the development of the untrammeled self.

To be sure, this student freedom was only freedom to be a student. As long as parents believed in certain mores, there were parietal rules and library fines and some fuss made over cheating at examinations or stealing books from the bookstore. But that was not because the university was tyrannical; it was because, rightly or wrongly, students were thought young and inexperienced and in need of guidance.

Earlier, student hostility and violence had been a recurrent problem. It seemed to be resolved by letting the student choose his courses and preparing him for them sooner. He became docile, which means teachable, and he was believed to acquiesce in the fact that he knew less than his teachers, did not own the university, and benefited from what it stood for.

Such was the institution that a couple of years' violence has made into an historical memory. True, the American university had begun to lose its soul through misguided public service, and students had grievances they should have analyzed and publicized. But by organizing hatred instead, by assaulting and imprisoning their teachers, dividing faculties into factions, turning weak heads into cowards and demagogues, ignoring the grave and legitimate causes for reform, advocating the bearing of arms on campus, and preferring "confrontation" to getting their own way, hostile students have ushered in the reactionary university of the future, medieval model.

For it is clear that once the traditions of deference and civility are broken they cannot be knit up again at will. No one can be sure of the future, but the past is not dumb. Medieval student power met its quietus when the aggressive traits of its leaders were, so to speak, taken over by the state. The students, losing their privilege, became subjects like any other and were put down.

Nobody with a heart and a mind can look forward to the fulfillment of either reactionary hope—it took so long to develop the republic of learning in which *study* was the sole aim and test of the institution! Who can bear to think of reliving 1266 and All That?

Article III – Presumptions in Civil Cases

Rule 301. Presumptions in Civil Cases Generally

In a civil case, unless a federal statute or these rules provide otherwise, the party against whom a presumption is directed has the burden of producing evidence to rebut the presumption. But this rule does not shift the burden of persuasion, which remains on the party who had it originally.

Rule 302. Applying State Law to Presumptions in Civil Cases

In a civil case, state law governs the effect of a presumption regarding a claim or defense for which state law supplies the rule of decision.

Article IV – Relevance and its Limits

Rule 401. Test for Relevant Evidence

Evidence is relevant if:

(a)   it has any tendency to make a fact more or less probable than it would be without the evidence; and

(b)   the fact is of consequence in determining the action.

Rule 402. General Admissibility of Relevant Evidence

Relevant evidence is admissible unless any of the following provides otherwise:

- the United States Constitution;
- a federal statute;
- these rules; or
- other rules prescribed by the Supreme Court.

Irrelevant evidence is not admissible.

Rule 403. Excluding Relevant Evidence for Prejudice, Confusion, Waste of Time, or Other Reasons

The court may exclude relevant evidence if its probative value is substantially outweighed by a danger of one or more of the following: unfair prejudice, confusing the issues, misleading the jury, undue delay, wasting time, or needlessly presenting cumulative evidence.

Rule 404. Character Evidence; Crimes or Other Acts

(a)   **Character Evidence**.

(1)   *Prohibited Uses.* Evidence of a person's character or character trait is not admissible to prove that on a particular occasion the person acted in accordance with the character or trait.

(2)   *Exceptions for a Defendant or Victim in a Criminal Case.* The following exceptions apply in a criminal case:

(A) a defendant may offer evidence of the defendant's pertinent trait, and if the evidence is admitted, the prosecutor may offer evidence to rebut it;

(B) subject to the limitations in Rule 412, a defendant may offer evidence of an alleged victim's pertinent trait, and if the evidence is admitted, the prosecutor may:

  (i) offer evidence to rebut it; and

  (ii) offer evidence of the defendant's same trait; and

(C) in a homicide case, the prosecutor may offer evidence of the alleged victim's trait of peacefulness to rebut evidence that the victim was the first aggressor.

(3) *Exceptions for a Witness*. Evidence of a witness's character may be admitted under Rules 607, 608, and 609.

(b) **Crimes, Wrongs, or Other Acts**.

(1) *Prohibited Uses*. Evidence of a crime, wrong, or other act is not admissible to prove a person's character in order to show that on a particular occasion the person acted in accordance with the character.

(2) *Permitted Uses; Notice in a Criminal Case*. This evidence may be admissible for another purpose, such as proving motive, opportunity, intent, preparation, plan, knowledge, identity, absence of mistake, or lack of accident. On request by a defendant in a criminal case, the prosecutor must:

  (A) provide reasonable notice of the general nature of any such evidence that the prosecutor intends to offer at trial; and

  (B) do so before trial — or during trial if the court, for good cause, excuses lack of pretrial notice.

Rule 405. Methods of Proving Character

(a) **By Reputation or Opinion**. When evidence of a person's character or character trait is admissible, it may be proved by testimony about the person's reputation or by testimony in the form of an opinion. On cross-examination of the character witness, the court may allow an inquiry into relevant specific instances of the person's conduct.

(b) **By Specific Instances of Conduct**. When a person's character or character trait is an essential element of a charge, claim, or defense, the character or trait may also be proved by relevant specific instances of the person's conduct.

Rule 406. Habit; Routine Practice

Evidence of a person's habit or an organization's routine practice may be admitted to prove that on a particular occasion the person or organization acted in accordance with the habit or routine practice. The court may admit this evidence regardless of whether it is corroborated or whether there was an eyewitness.

Rule 407. Subsequent Remedial Measures

When measures are taken that would have made an earlier injury or harm less likely to occur, evidence of the subsequent measures is not admissible to prove:

- negligence;
- culpable conduct;
- a defect in a product or its design; or
- a need for a warning or instruction.

But the court may admit this evidence for another purpose, such as impeachment or — if disputed — proving ownership, control, or the feasibility of precautionary measures.

Rule 408. Compromise Offers and Negotiations

(a) **Prohibited Uses.** Evidence of the following is not admissible — on behalf of any party — either to prove or disprove the validity or amount of a disputed claim or to impeach by a prior inconsistent statement or a contradiction:

    (1) furnishing, promising, or offering — or accepting, promising to accept, or offering to accept — a valuable consideration in compromising or attempting to compromise the claim; and

    (2) conduct or a statement made during compromise negotiations about the claim — except when offered in a criminal case and when the negotiations related to a claim by a public office in the exercise of its regulatory, investigative, or enforcement authority.

(b) **Exceptions.** The court may admit this evidence for another purpose, such as proving a witness's bias or prejudice, negating a contention of undue delay, or proving an effort to obstruct a criminal investigation or prosecution.

Rule 409. Offers to Pay Medical and Similar Expenses

Evidence of furnishing, promising to pay, or offering to pay medical, hospital, or similar expenses resulting from an injury is not admissible to prove liability for the injury.

Rule 410. Pleas, Plea Discussions, and Related Statements

(a) **Prohibited Uses**. In a civil or criminal case, evidence of the following is not admissible against the defendant who made the plea or participated in the plea discussions:
   (1)   a guilty plea that was later withdrawn;
   (2)   a nolo contendere plea;
   (3)   a statement made during a proceeding on either of those pleas under Federal Rule of Criminal Procedure 11 or a comparable state procedure; or
   (4)   a statement made during plea discussions with an attorney for the prosecuting authority if the discussions did not result in a guilty plea or they resulted in a later-withdrawn guilty plea.

(b) **Exceptions**. The court may admit a statement described in Rule 410(a)(3) or (4):
   (1)   in any proceeding in which another statement made during the same plea or plea discussions has been introduced, if in fairness the statements ought to be considered together; or
   (2)   in a criminal proceeding for perjury or false statement, if the defendant made the statement under oath, on the record, and with counsel present.

Rule 411. Liability Insurance

Evidence that a person was or was not insured against liability is not admissible to prove whether the person acted negligently or otherwise wrongfully. But the court may admit this evidence for another purpose, such as proving a witness's bias or prejudice or proving agency, ownership, or control.

Rule 412. Sex-Offense Cases: The Victim

(a) **Prohibited Uses**. The following evidence is not admissible in a civil or criminal proceeding involving alleged sexual misconduct:

(1) evidence offered to prove that a victim engaged in other sexual behavior; or

(2) evidence offered to prove a victim's sexual predisposition.

(b) **Exceptions**.

(1) *Criminal Cases*. The court may admit the following evidence in a criminal case:

(A) evidence of specific instances of a victim's sexual behavior, if offered to prove that someone other than the defendant was the source of semen, injury, or other physical evidence;

(B) evidence of specific instances of a victim's sexual behavior with respect to the person accused of the sexual misconduct, if offered by the defendant to prove consent or if offered by the prosecutor; and

(C) evidence whose exclusion would violate the defendant's constitutional rights.

(2) *Civil Cases*. In a civil case, the court may admit evidence offered to prove a victim's sexual behavior or sexual predisposition if its probative value substantially outweighs the danger of harm to any victim and of unfair prejudice to any party. The court may admit evidence of a victim's reputation only if the victim has placed it in controversy.

(c) **Procedure to Determine Admissibility**.

(1) *Motion*. If a party intends to offer evidence under Rule 412(b), the party must:

(A) file a motion that specifically describes the evidence and states the purpose for which it is to be offered;

(B) do so at least 14 days before trial unless the court, for good cause, sets a different time;

(C) serve the motion on all parties; and

(D) notify the victim or, when appropriate, the victim's guardian or representative.

(2) *Hearing*. Before admitting evidence under this rule, the court must conduct an in camera hearing and give the victim and parties a right to attend and be heard. Unless the court orders otherwise, the motion, related materials, and the record of the hearing must be and remain sealed.

(d) **Definition of "Victim."** In this rule, "victim" includes an alleged victim.

Rule 413. Similar Crimes in Sexual-Assault Cases

(a) **Permitted Uses**. In a criminal case in which a defendant is accused of a sexual assault, the court may admit evidence that the defendant committed any other sexual assault. The evidence may be considered on any matter to which it is relevant.

(b) **Disclosure to the Defendant**. If the prosecutor intends to offer this evidence, the prosecutor must disclose it to the defendant, including witnesses' statements or a summary of the expected testimony. The prosecutor must do so at least 15 days before trial or at a later time that the court allows for good cause.

(c) **Effect on Other Rules**. This rule does not limit the admission or consideration of evidence under any other rule.

(d) **Definition of "Sexual Assault."** In this rule and Rule 415, "sexual assault" means a crime under federal law or under state law (as "state" is defined in 18 U.S.C. § 513) involving:

   (1) any conduct prohibited by 18 U.S.C. chapter 109A;

   (2) contact, without consent, between any part of the defendant's body — or an object — and another person's genitals or anus;

   (3) contact, without consent, between the defendant's genitals or anus and any part of another person's body;

   (4) deriving sexual pleasure or gratification from inflicting death, bodily injury, or physical pain on another person; or

   (5) an attempt or conspiracy to engage in conduct described in subparagraphs (1)–(4).

Rule 414. Similar Crimes in Child Molestation Cases

(a) **Permitted Uses**. In a criminal case in which a defendant is accused of child molestation, the court may admit evidence that the defendant committed any other child molestation. The evidence may be considered on any matter to which it is relevant.

(b) **Disclosure to the Defendant**. If the prosecutor intends to offer this evidence, the prosecutor must disclose it to the defendant, including witnesses' statements or a summary of the expected testimony. The prosecutor must do so at least 15 days before trial or at a later time that the court allows for good cause.

(c) **Effect on Other Rules**. This rule does not limit the admission or consideration of evidence under any other rule.

(d) **Definition of "Child" and "Child Molestation."** In this rule and Rule 415:

    (1) "child" means a person below the age of 14; and

    (2) "child molestation" means a crime under federal law or under state law (as "state" is defined in 18 U.S.C. § 513) involving:

        (A) any conduct prohibited by 18 U.S.C. chapter 109A and committed with a child;

        (B) any conduct prohibited by 18 U.S.C. chapter 110;

        (C) contact between any part of the defendant's body — or an object — and a child's genitals or anus;

        (D) contact between the defendant's genitals or anus and any part of a child's body;

        (E) deriving sexual pleasure or gratification from inflicting death, bodily injury, or physical pain on a child; or

        (F) an attempt or conspiracy to engage in conduct described in subparagraphs (A)–(E).

Rule 415. Similar Acts in Civil Cases Involving Sexual Assault or Child Molestation

(a) **Permitted Uses**. In a civil case involving a claim for relief based on a party's alleged sexual assault or child molestation, the court may admit evidence that the party committed any other sexual assault or child molestation. The evidence may be considered as provided in Rules 413 and 414.

(b) **Disclosure to the Opponent**. If a party intends to offer this evidence, the party must disclose it to the party against whom it will be offered, including witnesses' statements or a summary of the expected testimony. The party must do so at least 15 days before trial or at a later time that the court allows for good cause.

(c) **Effect on Other Rules**. This rule does not limit the admission or consideration of evidence under any other rule.

Article V – Privileges

Rule 501. Privilege in General

The common law — as interpreted by United States courts in the light of reason and experience — governs a claim of privilege unless any of the following provides otherwise:

- the United States Constitution;
- a federal statute; or
- rules prescribed by the Supreme Court.

But in a civil case, state law governs privilege regarding a claim or defense for which state law supplies the rule of decision.

Rule 502. Attorney-Client Privilege and Work Product; Limitations on Waiver

The following provisions apply, in the circumstances set out, to disclosure of a communication or information covered by the attorney-client privilege or work-product protection.

(a) **Disclosure Made in a Federal Proceeding or to a Federal Office or Agency; Scope of a Waiver**. When the disclosure is made in a federal proceeding or to a federal office or agency and waives the attorney-client privilege or work-product protection, the waiver extends to an undisclosed communication or information in a federal or state proceeding only if:
   (1) the waiver is intentional;
   (2) the disclosed and undisclosed communications or information concern the same subject matter; and
   (3) they ought in fairness to be considered together.

(b) **Inadvertent Disclosure**. When made in a federal proceeding or to a federal office or agency, the disclosure does not operate as a waiver in a federal or state proceeding if:
   (1) the disclosure is inadvertent;
   (2) the holder of the privilege or protection took reasonable steps to prevent disclosure; and
   (3) the holder promptly took reasonable steps to rectify the error, including (if applicable) following Federal Rule of Civil Procedure 26 (b)(5)(B).

(c) **Disclosure Made in a State Proceeding**. When the disclosure is made in a state proceeding and is not the subject of a state-court order concerning waiver, the disclosure does not operate as a waiver in a federal proceeding if the disclosure:

    (1)   would not be a waiver under this rule if it had been made in a federal proceeding; or

    (2)   is not a waiver under the law of the state where the disclosure occurred.

(d) **Controlling Effect of a Court Order**. A federal court may order that the privilege or protection is not waived by disclosure connected with the litigation pending before the court — in which event the disclosure is also not a waiver in any other federal or state proceeding.

(e) **Controlling Effect of a Party Agreement**. An agreement on the effect of disclosure in a federal proceeding is binding only on the parties to the agreement, unless it is incorporated into a court order.

(f) **Controlling Effect of this Rule**. Notwithstanding Rules 101 and 1101, this rule applies to state proceedings and to federal court-annexed and federal court-mandated arbitration proceedings, in the circumstances set out in the rule. And notwithstanding Rule 501, this rule applies even if state law provides the rule of decision.

(g) **Definitions**. In this rule:

    (1)   "attorney-client privilege" means the protection that applicable law provides for confidential attorney-client communications; and

    (2)   "work-product protection" means the protection that applicable law provides for tangible material (or its intangible equivalent) prepared in anticipation of litigation or for trial.

Article VI – Witnesses

Rule 601. Competency to Testify in General

Every person is competent to be a witness unless these rules provide otherwise. But in a civil case, state law governs the witness's competency regarding a claim or defense for which state law supplies the rule of decision.

Rule 602. Need for Personal Knowledge

A witness may testify to a matter only if evidence is introduced sufficient to support a finding that the witness has personal knowledge of the matter. Evidence to prove personal knowledge may consist of the witness's own testimony. This rule does not apply to a witness's expert testimony under Rule 703.

Rule 603. Oath or Affirmation to Testify Truthfully

Before testifying, a witness must give an oath or affirmation to testify truthfully. It must be in a form designed to impress that duty on the witness's conscience.

Rule 604. Interpreter

An interpreter must be qualified and must give an oath or affirmation to make a true translation.

Rule 605. Judge

The presiding judge may not testify as a witness at the trial. A party need not object to preserve the issue.

Rule 606. Juror

(a) **At the Trial**. A juror may not testify as a witness before the other jurors at the trial. If a juror is called to testify, the court must give a party an opportunity to object outside the jury's presence.

(b) **During an Inquiry into the Validity of a Verdict or Indictment**.

    (1) Prohibited Testimony or Other Evidence. During an inquiry into the validity of a verdict or indictment, a juror may not

testify about any statement made or incident that occurred during the jury's deliberations; the effect of anything on that juror's or another juror's vote; or any juror's mental processes concerning the verdict or indictment. The court may not receive a juror's affidavit or evidence of a juror's statement on these matters.

(2) **Exceptions**. A juror may testify about whether:
   (A) extraneous prejudicial information was improperly brought to the jury's attention;
   (B) an outside influence was improperly brought to bear on any juror; or
   (C) a mistake was made in entering the verdict on the verdict form.

Rule 607. Who May Impeach a Witness

Any party, including the party that called the witness, may attack the witness's credibility.

Rule 608. A Witness

(a) **Reputation or Opinion Evidence**. A witness's credibility may be attacked or supported by testimony about the witness's reputation for having a character for truthfulness or untruthfulness, or by testimony in the form of an opinion about that character. But evidence of truthful character is admissible only after the witness's character for truthfulness has been attacked.

(b) **Specific Instances of Conduct**. Except for a criminal conviction under Rule 609, extrinsic evidence is not admissible to prove specific instances of a witness's conduct in order to attack or support the witness's character for truthfulness. But the court may, on cross-examination, allow them to be inquired into if they are probative of the character for truthfulness or untruthfulness of:
   (1) the witness; or
   (2) another witness whose character the witness being cross-examined has testified about.

By testifying on another matter, a witness does not waive any privilege against self-incrimination for testimony that relates only to the witness's character for truthfulness.

Rule 609. Impeachment by Evidence of a Criminal Conviction

(a) **In General**. The following rules apply to attacking a witness's character for truthfulness by evidence of a criminal conviction:

    (1) for a crime that, in the convicting jurisdiction, was punishable by death or by imprisonment for more than one year, the evidence:

        (A) must be admitted, subject to Rule 403, in a civil case or in a criminal case in which the witness is not a defendant; and

        (B) must be admitted in a criminal case in which the witness is a defendant, if the probative value of the evidence outweighs its prejudicial effect to that defendant; and

    (2) for any crime regardless of the punishment, the evidence must be admitted if the court can readily determine that establishing the elements of the crime required proving — or the witness's admitting — a dishonest act or false statement.

(b) **Limit on Using the Evidence After 10 Years**. This subdivision (b) applies if more than 10 years have passed since the witness's conviction or release from confinement for it, whichever is later. Evidence of the conviction is admissible only if:

    (1) its probative value, supported by specific facts and circumstances, substantially outweighs its prejudicial effect; and

    (2) the proponent gives an adverse party reasonable written notice of the intent to use it so that the party has a fair opportunity to contest its use.

(c) **Effect of a Pardon, Annulment, or Certificate of Rehabilitation**. Evidence of a conviction is not admissible if:

    (1) the conviction has been the subject of a pardon, annulment, certificate of rehabilitation, or other equivalent procedure based on a finding that the person has been rehabilitated, and the person has not been convicted of a later crime punishable by death or by imprisonment for more than one year; or

    (2) the conviction has been the subject of a pardon, annulment, or other equivalent procedure based on a finding of innocence.

(d) **Juvenile Adjudications**. Evidence of a juvenile adjudication is admissible under this rule only if:
   (1) it is offered in a criminal case;
   (2) the adjudication was of a witness other than the defendant;
   (3) an adult's conviction for that offense would be admissible to attack the adult's credibility; and
   (4) admitting the evidence is necessary to fairly determine guilt or innocence.
(e) **Pendency of an Appeal**. A conviction that satisfies this rule is admissible even if an appeal is pending. Evidence of the pendency is also admissible.

Rule 610. Religious Beliefs or Opinions

Evidence of a witness's religious beliefs or opinions is not admissible to attack or support the witness's credibility.

Rule 611. Mode and Order of Examining Witnesses and Presenting Evidence

(a) **Control by the Court; Purposes**. The court should exercise reasonable control over the mode and order of examining witnesses and presenting evidence so as to:
   (1) make those procedures effective for determining the truth;
   (2) avoid wasting time; and
   (3) protect witnesses from harassment or undue embarrassment.
(b) **Scope of Cross-Examination**. Cross-examination should not go beyond the subject matter of the direct examination and matters affecting the witness's credibility. The court may allow inquiry into additional matters as if on direct examination.
(c) **Leading Questions**. Leading questions should not be used on direct examination except as necessary to develop the witness's testimony. Ordinarily, the court should allow leading questions:
   (1) on cross-examination; and
   (2) when a party calls a hostile witness, an adverse party, or a witness identified with an adverse party.

Rule 612. Writing Used to Refresh a Witness

(a) **Scope**. This rule gives an adverse party certain options when a witness uses a writing to refresh memory:

    (1) while testifying; or

    (2) before testifying, if the court decides that justice requires the party to have those options.

(b) **Adverse Party's Options; Deleting Unrelated Matter**. Unless 18 U.S.C. § 3500 provides otherwise in a criminal case, an adverse party is entitled to have the writing produced at the hearing, to inspect it, to cross-examine the witness about it, and to introduce in evidence any portion that relates to the witness's testimony. If the producing party claims that the writing includes unrelated matter, the court must examine the writing in camera, delete any unrelated portion, and order that the rest be delivered to the adverse party. Any portion deleted over objection must be preserved for the record.

(c) **Failure to Produce or Deliver the Writing**. If a writing is not produced or is not delivered as ordered, the court may issue any appropriate order. But if the prosecution does not comply in a criminal case, the court must strike the witness's testimony or — if justice so requires — declare a mistrial.

Rule 613. Witness

(a) **Showing or Disclosing the Statement During Examination**. When examining a witness about the witness's prior statement, a party need not show it or disclose its contents to the witness. But the party must, on request, show it or disclose its contents to an adverse party's attorney.

(b) **Extrinsic Evidence of a Prior Inconsistent Statement**. Extrinsic evidence of a witness's prior inconsistent statement is admissible only if the witness is given an opportunity to explain or deny the statement and an adverse party is given an opportunity to examine the witness about it, or if justice so requires. This subdivision (b) does not apply to an opposing party's statement under Rule 801(d)(2).

Rule 614. Court

(a) **Calling**. The court may call a witness on its own or at a party's request. Each party is entitled to cross-examine the witness.

(b) **Examining**. The court may examine a witness regardless of who calls the witness.

(c) **Objections**. A party may object to the court's calling or examining a witness either at that time or at the next opportunity when the jury is not present.

Rule 615. Excluding Witnesses

At a party's request, the court must order witnesses excluded so that they cannot hear other witnesses' testimony. Or the court may do so on its own. But this rule does not authorize excluding:

(a) a party who is a natural person;

(b) an officer or employee of a party that is not a natural person, after being designated as the party's representative by its attorney;

(c) a person whose presence a party shows to be essential to presenting the party's claim or defense; or

(d) a person authorized by statute to be present.

Article VII – Opinions and Expert Testimony

Rule 701. Opinion Testimony by Lay Witnesses

If a witness is not testifying as an expert, testimony in the form of an opinion is limited to one that is:

(a) rationally based on the witness's perception;

(b) helpful to clearly understanding the witness's testimony or to determining a fact in issue; and

(c) not based on scientific, technical, or other specialized knowledge within the scope of Rule 702.

Rule 702. Testimony by Expert Witnesses

A witness who is qualified as an expert by knowledge, skill, experience, training, or education may testify in the form of an opinion or otherwise if:

(a) the expert's scientific, technical, or other specialized knowledge will help the trier of fact to understand the evidence or to determine a fact in issue;

(b) the testimony is based on sufficient facts or data;

(c) the testimony is the product of reliable principles and methods; and

(d) the expert has reliably applied the principles and methods to the facts of the case.

Rule 703. Bases of an Expert

An expert may base an opinion on facts or data in the case that the expert has been made aware of or personally observed. If experts in the particular field would reasonably rely on those kinds of facts or data in forming an opinion on the subject, they need not be admissible for the opinion to be admitted. But if the facts or data would otherwise be inadmissible, the proponent of the opinion may disclose them to the jury only if their probative value in helping the jury evaluate the opinion substantially outweighs their prejudicial effect.

Rule 704. Opinion on an Ultimate Issue

(a) **In General — Not Automatically Objectionable**. An opinion is not objectionable just because it embraces an ultimate issue.

(b) **Exception**. In a criminal case, an expert witness must not state an opinion about whether the defendant did or did not have a mental state or condition that constitutes an element of the crime charged or of a defense. Those matters are for the trier of fact alone.

Rule 705. Disclosing the Facts or Data Underlying an Expert

Unless the court orders otherwise, an expert may state an opinion — and give the reasons for it — without first testifying to the underlying facts or data. But the expert may be required to disclose those facts or data on cross-examination.

Rule 706. Court-Appointed Expert Witnesses

(a) **Appointment Process**. On a party's motion or on its own, the court may order the parties to show cause why expert witnesses should not be appointed and may ask the parties to submit nominations. The court may appoint any expert that the parties agree on and any of its own choosing. But the court may only appoint someone who consents to act.

(b) **Expert's Role**. The court must inform the expert of the expert's duties. The court may do so in writing and have a copy filed with the clerk or may do so orally at a conference in which the parties have an opportunity to participate. The expert:
    (1) must advise the parties of any findings the expert makes;
    (2) may be deposed by any party;
    (3) may be called to testify by the court or any party; and
    (4) may be cross-examined by any party, including the party that called the expert.

(c) **Compensation**. The expert is entitled to a reasonable compensation, as set by the court. The compensation is payable as follows:
    (1) in a criminal case or in a civil case involving just compensation under the Fifth Amendment, from any funds that are provided by law; and

      (2)   in any other civil case, by the parties in the proportion and at the time that the court directs — and the compensation is then charged like other costs.

(d) **Disclosing the Appointment to the Jury**. The court may authorize disclosure to the jury that the court appointed the expert.

(e) **Parties' Choice of Their Own Experts**. This rule does not limit a party in calling its own experts.

Article VIII – Hearsay

Rule 801. Definitions That Apply to This Article; Exclusions from Hearsay

The following definitions apply under this article:

(a) **Statement**. "Statement" means a person's oral assertion, written assertion, or nonverbal conduct, if the person intended it as an assertion.

(b) **Declarant**. "Declarant" means the person who made the statement.

(c) **Hearsay**. "Hearsay" means a statement that:
  (1) the declarant does not make while testifying at the current trial or hearing; and
  (2) a party offers in evidence to prove the truth of the matter asserted in the statement.

(d) **Statements That Are Not Hearsay**. A statement that meets the following conditions is not hearsay:
  (1) *A Declarant-Witness's Prior Statement*. The declarant testifies and is subject to cross-examination about a prior statement, and the statement:
    (A) is inconsistent with the declarant's testimony and was given under penalty of perjury at a trial, hearing, or other proceeding or in a deposition;
    (B) is consistent with the declarant's testimony and is offered:
      (i) to rebut an express or implied charge that the declarant recently fabricated it or acted from a recent improper influence or motive in so testifying; or
      (ii) to rehabilitate the declarant's credibility as a witness when attacked on another ground; or
    (C) identifies a person as someone the declarant perceived earlier.
  (2) *An Opposing Party's Statement*. The statement is offered against an opposing party and:
    (A) was made by the party in an individual or representative capacity;
    (B) is one the party manifested that it adopted or believed to be true;

(C) was made by a person whom the party authorized to make a statement on the subject;

(D) was made by the party's agent or employee on a matter within the scope of that relationship and while it existed; or

(E) was made by the party's coconspirator during and in furtherance of the conspiracy.

The statement must be considered but does not by itself establish the declarant's authority under (C); the existence or scope of the relationship under (D); or the existence of the conspiracy or participation in it under (E).

Rule 802. The Rule Against Hearsay

Hearsay is not admissible unless any of the following provides otherwise:

- a federal statute;
- these rules; or
- other rules prescribed by the Supreme Court.

Rule 803. Exceptions to the Rule Against Hearsay

The following are not excluded by the rule against hearsay, regardless of whether the declarant is available as a witness:

(1) **Present Sense Impression**. A statement describing or explaining an event or condition, made while or immediately after the declarant perceived it.

(2) **Excited Utterance**. A statement relating to a startling event or condition, made while the declarant was under the stress of excitement that it caused.

(3) **Then-Existing Mental, Emotional, or Physical Condition**. A statement of the declarant's then-existing state of mind (such as motive, intent, or plan) or emotional, sensory, or physical condition (such as mental feeling, pain, or bodily health), but not including a statement of memory or belief to prove the fact remembered or believed unless it relates to the validity or terms of the declarant's will.

(4) **Statement Made for Medical Diagnosis or Treatment**. A statement that:

(A) is made for — and is reasonably pertinent to — medical diagnosis or treatment; and

(B) describes medical history; past or present symptoms or sensations; their inception; or their general cause.

(5) **Recorded Recollection**. A record that:

(A) is on a matter the witness once knew about but now cannot recall well enough to testify fully and accurately;

(B) was made or adopted by the witness when the matter was fresh in the witness's memory; and

(C) accurately reflects the witness's knowledge.

If admitted, the record may be read into evidence but may be received as an exhibit only if offered by an adverse party.

(6) **Records of a Regularly Conducted Activity**. A record of an act, event, condition, opinion, or diagnosis if:

(A) the record was made at or near the time by — or from information transmitted by — someone with knowledge;

(B) the record was kept in the course of a regularly conducted activity of a business, organization, occupation, or calling, whether or not for profit;

(C) making the record was a regular practice of that activity;

(D) all these conditions are shown by the testimony of the custodian or another qualified witness, or by a certification that complies with Rule 902(11) or (12) or with a statute permitting certification; and

(E) the opponent does not show that the source of information or the method or circumstances of preparation indicate a lack of trustworthiness.

(7) **Absence of a Record of a Regularly Conducted Activity**. Evidence that a matter is not included in a record described in paragraph (6) if:

(A) the evidence is admitted to prove that the matter did not occur or exist;

(B) a record was regularly kept for a matter of that kind; and

(C) the opponent does not show that the possible source of the information or other circumstances indicate a lack of trustworthiness.

(8) **Public Records**. A record or statement of a public office if:
    (A) it sets out:
        (i) the office's activities;
        (ii) a matter observed while under a legal duty to report, but not including, in a criminal case, a matter observed by law-enforcement personnel; or
        (iii) in a civil case or against the government in a criminal case, factual findings from a legally authorized investigation; and
    (B) the opponent does not show that the source of information or other circumstances indicate a lack of trustworthiness.

(9) **Public Records of Vital Statistics**. A record of a birth, death, or marriage, if reported to a public office in accordance with a legal duty.

(10) **Absence of a Public Record**. Testimony — or a certification under Rule 902 — that a diligent search failed to disclose a public record or statement if:
    (A) the testimony or certification is admitted to prove that
        (i) the record or statement does not exist; or
        (ii) a matter did not occur or exist, if a public office regularly kept a record or statement for a matter of that kind; and
    (B) in a criminal case, a prosecutor who intends to offer a certification provides written notice of that intent at least 14 days before trial, and the defendant does not object in writing within 7 days of receiving the notice — unless the court sets a different time for the notice or the objection.

(11) **Records of Religious Organizations Concerning Personal or Family History**. A statement of birth, legitimacy, ancestry, marriage, divorce, death, relationship by blood or marriage, or similar facts of personal or family history, contained in a regularly kept record of a religious organization.

(12) **Certificates of Marriage, Baptism, and Similar Ceremonies**. A statement of fact contained in a certificate:
   (A) made by a person who is authorized by a religious organization or by law to perform the act certified;
   (B) attesting that the person performed a marriage or similar ceremony or administered a sacrament; and
   (C) purporting to have been issued at the time of the act or within a reasonable time after it.

(13) **Family Records**. A statement of fact about personal or family history contained in a family record, such as a Bible, genealogy, chart, engraving on a ring, inscription on a portrait, or engraving on an urn or burial marker.

(14) **Records of Documents That Affect an Interest in Property**. The record of a document that purports to establish or affect an interest in property if:
   (A) the record is admitted to prove the content of the original recorded document, along with its signing and its delivery by each person who purports to have signed it;
   (B) the record is kept in a public office; and
   (C) a statute authorizes recording documents of that kind in that office.

(15) **Statements in Documents That Affect an Interest in Property**. A statement contained in a document that purports to establish or affect an interest in property if the matter stated was relevant to the document's purpose — unless later dealings with the property are inconsistent with the truth of the statement or the purport of the document.

(16) **Statements in Ancient Documents**. A statement in a document that is at least 20 years old and whose authenticity is established.

(17) **Market Reports and Similar Commercial Publications**. Market quotations, lists, directories, or other compilations that are generally relied on by the public or by persons in particular occupations.

(18) **Statements in Learned Treatises, Periodicals, or Pamphlets**. A statement contained in a treatise, periodical, or pamphlet if:

(A) the statement is called to the attention of an expert witness on cross-examination or relied on by the expert on direct examination; and

(B) the publication is established as a reliable authority by the expert's admission or testimony, by another expert's testimony, or by judicial notice.

If admitted, the statement may be read into evidence but not received as an exhibit.

(19) **Reputation Concerning Personal or Family History**. A reputation among a person's family by blood, adoption, or marriage — or among a person's associates or in the community — concerning the person's birth, adoption, legitimacy, ancestry, marriage, divorce, death, relationship by blood, adoption, or marriage, or similar facts of personal or family history.

(20) **Reputation Concerning Boundaries or General History**. A reputation in a community — arising before the controversy — concerning boundaries of land in the community or customs that affect the land, or concerning general historical events important to that community, state, or nation.

(21) **Reputation Concerning Character**. A reputation among a person's associates or in the community concerning the person's character.

(22) **Judgment of a Previous Conviction**. Evidence of a final judgment of conviction if:

(A) the judgment was entered after a trial or guilty plea, but not a nolo contendere plea;

(B) the conviction was for a crime punishable by death or by imprisonment for more than a year;

(C) the evidence is admitted to prove any fact essential to the judgment; and

(D) when offered by the prosecutor in a criminal case for a purpose other than impeachment, the judgment was against the defendant.

The pendency of an appeal may be shown but does not affect admissibility.

(23) **Judgments Involving Personal, Family, or General History, or a Boundary**. A judgment that is admitted to

prove a matter of personal, family, or general history, or boundaries, if the matter:

(A) was essential to the judgment; and

(B) could be proved by evidence of reputation.

(24) [Other Exceptions .] [Transferred to Rule 807.]

Rule 804. Hearsay Exceptions; Declarant Unavailable

(a) **Criteria for Being Unavailable**. A declarant is considered to be unavailable as a witness if the declarant:

(1) is exempted from testifying about the subject matter of the declarant's statement because the court rules that a privilege applies;

(2) refuses to testify about the subject matter despite a court order to do so;

(3) testifies to not remembering the subject matter;

(4) cannot be present or testify at the trial or hearing because of death or a then-existing infirmity, physical illness, or mental illness; or

(5) is absent from the trial or hearing and the statement's proponent has not been able, by process or other reasonable means, to procure:

(A) the declarant's attendance, in the case of a hearsay exception under Rule 804(b)(1) or (6); or

(B) the declarant's attendance or testimony, in the case of a hearsay exception under Rule 804(b)(2), (3), or (4).

But this subdivision (a) does not apply if the statement's proponent procured or wrongfully caused the declarant's unavailability as a witness in order to prevent the declarant from attending or testifying.

(b) **The Exceptions**. The following are not excluded by the rule against hearsay if the declarant is unavailable as a witness:

(1) *Former Testimony*. Testimony that:

(A) was given as a witness at a trial, hearing, or lawful deposition, whether given during the current proceeding or a different one; and

(B) is now offered against a party who had — or, in a civil case, whose predecessor in interest had — an opportunity and similar motive to develop it by direct, cross-, or redirect examination.

(2) *Statement Under the Belief of Imminent Death.* In a prosecution for homicide or in a civil case, a statement that the declarant, while believing the declarant's death to be imminent, made about its cause or circumstances.

(3) *Statement Against Interest.* A statement that:

    (A) a reasonable person in the declarant's position would have made only if the person believed it to be true because, when made, it was so contrary to the declarant's proprietary or pecuniary interest or had so great a tendency to invalidate the declarant's claim against someone else or to expose the declarant to civil or criminal liability; and

    (B) is supported by corroborating circumstances that clearly indicate its trustworthiness, if it is offered in a criminal case as one that tends to expose the declarant to criminal liability.

(4) *Statement of Personal or Family History.* A statement about:

    (A) the declarant's own birth, adoption, legitimacy, ancestry, marriage, divorce, relationship by blood, adoption, or marriage, or similar facts of personal or family history, even though the declarant had no way of acquiring personal knowledge about that fact; or

    (B) another person concerning any of these facts, as well as death, if the declarant was related to the person by blood, adoption, or marriage or was so intimately associated with the person's family that the declarant's information is likely to be accurate.

(5) [Other Exceptions .] [Transferred to Rule 807.]

(6) *Statement Offered Against a Party That Wrongfully Caused the Declarant's Unavailability.* A statement offered against a party that wrongfully caused — or acquiesced in wrongfully causing — the declarant's unavailability as a witness, and did so intending that result.

Rule 805. Hearsay Within Hearsay

Hearsay within hearsay is not excluded by the rule against hearsay if each part of the combined statements conforms with an exception to the rule.

Rule 806. Attacking and Supporting the Declarant

When a hearsay statement — or a statement described in Rule 801(d)(2)(C), (D), or (E) — has been admitted in evidence, the declarant's credibility may be attacked, and then supported, by any evidence that would be admissible for those purposes if the declarant had testified as a witness. The court may admit evidence of the declarant's inconsistent statement or conduct, regardless of when it occurred or whether the declarant had an opportunity to explain or deny it. If the party against whom the statement was admitted calls the declarant as a witness, the party may examine the declarant on the statement as if on cross-examination.

Rule 807. Residual Exception

(a) **In General**. Under the following circumstances, a hearsay statement is not excluded by the rule against hearsay even if the statement is not specifically covered by a hearsay exception in Rule 803 or 804:

    (1) the statement has equivalent circumstantial guarantees of trustworthiness;

    (2) it is offered as evidence of a material fact;

    (3) it is more probative on the point for which it is offered than any other evidence that the proponent can obtain through reasonable efforts; and

    (4) admitting it will best serve the purposes of these rules and the interests of justice.

(b) **Notice**. The statement is admissible only if, before the trial or hearing, the proponent gives an adverse party reasonable notice of the intent to offer the statement and its particulars, including the declarant's name and address, so that the party has a fair opportunity to meet it.

Article IX – Authentication and Identification

Rule 901. Authenticating or Identifying Evidence

(a) **In General**. To satisfy the requirement of authenticating or identifying an item of evidence, the proponent must produce evidence sufficient to support a finding that the item is what the proponent claims it is.

(b) **Examples**. The following are examples only — not a complete list — of evidence that satisfies the requirement:

   (1) *Testimony of a Witness with Knowledge*. Testimony that an item is what it is claimed to be.

   (2) *Nonexpert Opinion About Handwriting*. A nonexpert's opinion that handwriting is genuine, based on a familiarity with it that was not acquired for the current litigation.

   (3) *Comparison by an Expert Witness or the Trier of Fact*. A comparison with an authenticated specimen by an expert witness or the trier of fact.

   (4) *Distinctive Characteristics and the Like*. The appearance, contents, substance, internal patterns, or other distinctive characteristics of the item, taken together with all the circumstances.

   (5) *Opinion About a Voice*. An opinion identifying a person's voice — whether heard firsthand or through mechanical or electronic transmission or recording — based on hearing the voice at any time under circumstances that connect it with the alleged speaker.

   (6) *Evidence About a Telephone Conversation*. For a telephone conversation, evidence that a call was made to the number assigned at the time to:

      (A) a particular person, if circumstances, including self-identification, show that the person answering was the one called; or

      (B) a particular business, if the call was made to a business and the call related to business reasonably transacted over the telephone.

   (7) *Evidence About Public Records*. Evidence that:

      (A) a document was recorded or filed in a public office as authorized by law; or

    (B) a purported public record or statement is from the office where items of this kind are kept.

(8) *Evidence About Ancient Documents or Data Compilations.* For a document or data compilation, evidence that it:

    (A) is in a condition that creates no suspicion about its authenticity;

    (B) was in a place where, if authentic, it would likely be; and

    (C) is at least 20 years old when offered.

(9) *Evidence About a Process or System.* Evidence describing a process or system and showing that it produces an accurate result.

(10) *Methods Provided by a Statute or Rule.* Any method of authentication or identification allowed by a federal statute or a rule prescribed by the Supreme Court.

Rule 902. Evidence That Is Self-Authenticating

The following items of evidence are self-authenticating; they require no extrinsic evidence of authenticity in order to be admitted:

(1) **Domestic Public Documents That Are Sealed and Signed**. A document that bears:

    (A) a seal purporting to be that of the United States; any state, district, commonwealth, territory, or insular possession of the United States; the former Panama Canal Zone; the Trust Territory of the Pacific Islands; a political subdivision of any of these entities; or a department, agency, or officer of any entity named above; and

    (B) a signature purporting to be an execution or attestation.

(2) **Domestic Public Documents That Are Not Sealed but Are Signed and Certified**. A document that bears no seal if:

    (A) it bears the signature of an officer or employee of an entity named in Rule 902(1)(A); and

    (B) another public officer who has a seal and official duties within that same entity certifies under seal — or its equivalent — that the signer has the official capacity and that the signature is genuine.

(3) **Foreign Public Documents**. A document that purports to be signed or attested by a person who is authorized by a foreign country's law to do so. The document must be accompanied by a final certification that certifies the genuineness of the signature and official position of the signer or attester — or of any foreign official whose certificate of genuineness relates to the signature or attestation or is in a chain of certificates of genuineness relating to the signature or attestation. The certification may be made by a secretary of a United States embassy or legation; by a consul general, vice consul, or consular agent of the United States; or by a diplomatic or consular official of the foreign country assigned or accredited to the United States. If all parties have been given a reasonable opportunity to investigate the document's authenticity and accuracy, the court may, for good cause, either:

(A) order that it be treated as presumptively authentic without final certification; or

(B) allow it to be evidenced by an attested summary with or without final certification.

(4) **Certified Copies of Public Records**. A copy of an official record — or a copy of a document that was recorded or filed in a public office as authorized by law — if the copy is certified as correct by:

(A) the custodian or another person authorized to make the certification; or

(B) a certificate that complies with Rule 902(1), (2), or (3), a federal statute, or a rule prescribed by the Supreme Court.

(5) **Official Publications**. A book, pamphlet, or other publication purporting to be issued by a public authority.

(6) **Newspapers and Periodicals**. Printed material purporting to be a newspaper or periodical.

(7) **Trade Inscriptions and the Like**. An inscription, sign, tag, or label purporting to have been affixed in the course of business and indicating origin, ownership, or control.

(8) **Acknowledged Documents**. A document accompanied by a certificate of acknowledgment that is lawfully executed by a notary public or another officer who is authorized to take acknowledgments.

(9) **Commercial Paper and Related Documents**. Commercial paper, a signature on it, and related documents, to the extent allowed by general commercial law.

(10) **Presumptions Under a Federal Statute**. A signature, document, or anything else that a federal statute declares to be presumptively or prima facie genuine or authentic.

(11) **Certified Domestic Records of a Regularly Conducted Activity**. The original or a copy of a domestic record that meets the requirements of Rule 803(6)(A)-(C), as shown by a certification of the custodian or another qualified person that complies with a federal statute or a rule prescribed by the Supreme Court. Before the trial or hearing, the proponent must give an adverse party reasonable written notice of the intent to offer the record — and must make the record and certification available for inspection — so that the party has a fair opportunity to challenge them.

(12) **Certified Foreign Records of a Regularly Conducted Activity**. In a civil case, the original or a copy of a foreign record that meets the requirements of Rule 902(11), modified as follows: the certification, rather than complying with a federal statute or Supreme Court rule, must be signed in a manner that, if falsely made, would subject the maker to a criminal penalty in the country where the certification is signed. The proponent must also meet the notice requirements of Rule 902(11).

Rule 903. Subscribing Witness

A subscribing witness's testimony is necessary to authenticate a writing only if required by the law of the jurisdiction that governs its validity.

Article X – Contents of Writings, Recordings, and Photographs

Rule 1001. Definitions That Apply to This Article

In this article:

(a) A "writing" consists of letters, words, numbers, or their equivalent set down in any form.

(b) A "recording" consists of letters, words, numbers, or their equivalent recorded in any manner.

(c) A "photograph" means a photographic image or its equivalent stored in any form.

(d) An "original" of a writing or recording means the writing or recording itself or any counterpart intended to have the same effect by the person who executed or issued it. For electronically stored information, "original" means any printout — or other output readable by sight — if it accurately reflects the information. An "original" of a photograph includes the negative or a print from it.

(e) A "duplicate" means a counterpart produced by a mechanical, photographic, chemical, electronic, or other equivalent process or technique that accurately reproduces the original.

Rule 1002. Requirement of the Original

An original writing, recording, or photograph is required in order to prove its content unless these rules or a federal statute provides otherwise.

Rule 1003. Admissibility of Duplicates

A duplicate is admissible to the same extent as the original unless a genuine question is raised about the original's authenticity or the circumstances make it unfair to admit the duplicate.

Rule 1004. Admissibility of Other Evidence of Content

An original is not required and other evidence of the content of a writing, recording, or photograph is admissible if:

(a) all the originals are lost or destroyed, and not by the proponent acting in bad faith;

(b) an original cannot be obtained by any available judicial process;

(c) the party against whom the original would be offered had control of the original; was at that time put on notice, by pleadings or otherwise, that the original would be a subject of proof at the trial or hearing; and fails to produce it at the trial or hearing; or

(d) the writing, recording, or photograph is not closely related to a controlling issue.

Rule 1005. Copies of Public Records to Prove Content

The proponent may use a copy to prove the content of an official record — or of a document that was recorded or filed in a public office as authorized by law — if these conditions are met: the record or document is otherwise admissible; and the copy is certified as correct in accordance with Rule 902(4) or is testified to be correct by a witness who has compared it with the original. If no such copy can be obtained by reasonable diligence, then the proponent may use other evidence to prove the content.

Rule 1006. Summaries to Prove Content

The proponent may use a summary, chart, or calculation to prove the content of voluminous writings, recordings, or photographs that cannot be conveniently examined in court. The proponent must make the originals or duplicates available for examination or copying, or both, by other parties at a reasonable time and place. And the court may order the proponent to produce them in court.

Rule 1007. Testimony or Statement of a Party to Prove Content

The proponent may prove the content of a writing, recording, or photograph by the testimony, deposition, or written statement of the party against whom the evidence is offered. The proponent need not account for the original.

Rule 1008. Functions of the Court and Jury

Ordinarily, the court determines whether the proponent has fulfilled the factual conditions for admitting other evidence of the content of a writing, recording, or photograph under Rule 1004 or 1005. But in a jury trial, the jury determines — in accordance with Rule 104(b) — any issue about whether:

(a)   an asserted writing, recording, or photograph ever existed;
(b)   another one produced at the trial or hearing is the original; or
(c)   other evidence of content accurately reflects the content.

Article XI – Miscellaneous Rules

Rule 1101. Applicability of the Rules

(a) **To Courts and Judges**. These rules apply to proceedings before:
- United States district courts;
- United States bankruptcy and magistrate judges;
- United States courts of appeals;
- the United States Court of Federal Claims; and
- the district courts of Guam, the Virgin Islands, and the Northern Mariana Islands.

(b) **To Cases and Proceedings**. These rules apply in:
- civil cases and proceedings, including bankruptcy, admiralty, and maritime cases;
- criminal cases and proceedings; and
- contempt proceedings, except those in which the court may act summarily.

(c) **Rules on Privilege**. The rules on privilege apply to all stages of a case or proceeding.

(d) **Exceptions**. These rules — except for those on privilege — do not apply to the following:
  (1) the court's determination, under Rule 104(a), on a preliminary question of fact governing admissibility;
  (2) grand-jury proceedings; and
  (3) miscellaneous proceedings such as:
- extradition or rendition;
- issuing an arrest warrant, criminal summons, or search warrant;
- a preliminary examination in a criminal case;
- sentencing;
- granting or revoking probation or supervised release; and
- considering whether to release on bail or otherwise.

(e) **Other Statutes and Rules**. A federal statute or a rule prescribed by the Supreme Court may provide for admitting or excluding evidence independently from these rules.

Rule 1102. Amendments

These rules may be amended as provided in 28 U.S.C. § 2072.

Rule 1103. Title

These rules may be cited as the Federal Rules of Evidence.

Made in the USA
Middletown, DE
16 August 2017